Smiling Blind
A Marriage of Lies and Illusion

BY DORI B. HIGHTOWER

Cover art portrait of Dori by Franco Accornero.
Cover design and typesetting by Caron Dickinson.

Library of Congress Control Number: 2017912970
Published in the United States of America.

Smiling Blind
A Marriage of Lies and Illusion

INDEX

Dedications

My story is dedicated to all the women and men in relationships
who have been conned, destroyed, and survived to tell their stories.
You are not alone.

And to

President Barack Obama and First Lady Michelle Obama —
your leadership, despite so many obstacles and challenges,
has been extraordinary.

And to

Moe — pure unconditional love.

To the Reader

This is my memoir and story. All of the characters and events depicted are based upon my recollection of events, the public record, notes, documents and emails I found while I lived at Fleur D'Eau — my home with Dennis F. Hightower — and interviews of others who were present at one time or another over the last eight years. It was not easy for me to sort out fact from fiction during some of the years depicted in this story and to understand where the truth ended and a reality manufactured by my husband began.

A voluminous official record also exists as a result of the litigation between Dennis and me. There are thousands of pages of depositions, which include exhibits and hearing transcripts. Now there is also, finally, a divorce trial transcript!

In a few instances, I have changed the names of women who may or may not have been informed participants in a much larger story.

Acknowledgments

Thank you, God — without my faith, I would not exist.

There are so many people who have been part of this chapter of my life who helped me survive.

Thank you to my parents, Melvin and Jean Bye. You have been the best parents anyone could hope for. You are my everything and my greatest supporters. To my beautiful daughter inside and out, Brooke — you are my inspiration. To my incredible friend Lisa Nkonoki, family advocate and divorce/life coach extraordinaire, who suggested I write a book and supported me throughout this project.

To my sister from another mother, Helen Levy Koven. Your gifts are your ability to love and execute — you are extraordinary; and Dr. Richard Koven, Moe's vet and dog whisperer — thank you for taking care of my Moe Moe. You and Helen have been such an incredible blessing to my life.

To my friend Dee, thank you for your brilliant mind, your patience and kindness.

To Erin and Nadja, my stalwart allies, who supported me in every way to build my legal practice under the most challenging circumstances and conditions.

Thank you to my sister Rocki, who has taught me compassion and forgiveness. To my clients, I so appreciate and learn from each of you. And to my mentor, Justice Lubbie Harper, Jr., thank you is not enough — we know what we know.

Special thanks also to Caroline and to Victoria Helwig for their special talents, Chris Bosak for his editing expertise, Caron Dickinson for her phenomenal graphic design work and the fine artist Franco Accornero, who was always able to see, and for his beautiful art.

"A lie keeps growing and growing
until it's as plain as
the nose on your face."

—*Pinocchio*

THROUGH THE LOOKING GLASS

"I'm going to visit my son in Guatemala for a week or two," my husband told me suddenly, shortly after lunch. He had just emerged from his study for the first time all day, a common occurrence that summer.

"You're just going? Don't people who are married discuss things like that?" I asked, my hand shaking as I set my teacup down on the table. "What's going on with you?"

He was silent.

"I guess you don't want to be married anymore," I added, the words spilling out of my mouth before I could even think them through.

"Actually, yes, I want a divorce."

"Excuse me?"

"Nothing has turned out the way it was supposed to, Dori," he continued. His voice was blunt and empty, like his words meant nothing to him; like I meant nothing to him. "Let's just cut our losses now."

I struggled to catch my breath. Cut our losses? Where was this coming from?

"Why? What happened? Can we try seeing a counselor first?" I asked him, grasping for answers that did not exist. "Is this really what you want?"

He turned his back.

CHAPTER 1
ONCE UPON A TIME

April, 2009

"You didn't do your hair?" Lisa asked as she climbed into my little red rental car. "Really, Dori?"

I had tried to do my hair, but it had not worked out as planned. The April evening was humid and rainy, and the clouds followed us, wet and heavy, as we made our way into Midtown Manhattan. Beside me in the padded velour passenger seat, Lisa talked happily, proudly even, of the man awaiting us at the London Hotel: Dennis F. Hightower.

As she rattled off the list of Dennis' accomplishments — Harvard Business School graduate, Vietnam war hero complete with two bronze stars and a purple heart, a former high-ranking Walt Disney Company executive, the list went on and on — my mind was still back in the office. I was interested, however, in what sort of man could have prompted her to arrange this sort of meeting. Lisa was not the type to be easily star-struck.

I knew she had met Dennis at an award ceremony where he was an honoree. Dennis had come to New York City to attend a board meeting for Accenture, one of the most successful business consulting firms in the world. While Dennis was in the city, Lisa had managed to claim him for the evening so she could chaperone a little "meet and greet" for him and a couple of her most eligible friends. When her other friend had backed out, it became just the two of us heading into the city.

Lisa is a successful life coach and family advocate. More importantly, she had been my close friend for more than twenty years, ever since the day we struck up a conversation while waiting in line at a Boston Market in Hartford, Connecticut.

In Lisa's eyes, Dennis was a regular tycoon. The real deal. Accenture was just one of the many prestigious companies where he had held board positions, including TJX Companies, PanAmSat, PVH Corp., Northwest Airlines, The Gillette Company, Domino's Pizza, Brown Capital Management and Casey Family Programs, a national foundation focused on foster care and child welfare. He had served on the Chairman's Advisory Council at Price Waterhouse and on the Defense Business Board that provides business expertise to the U.S. Department of Defense.

It was a formidable list. These coveted positions were a badge of success and a mark of global power. They also came with a full roster of perks — restricted stock options, international travel and unparalleled access to global business leaders. I remembered reading that African-American men hold less than six percent of all positions on boards of Fortune 500 companies, making Dennis' achievements all the more impressive in my eyes.

Lisa had already emailed me this background information about Dennis. She figured I would want to study up before we met, but I had not had a chance to look at it. I could not remember ever hearing his name before, nor was I especially interested in reading about him in advance of our meeting. Still, I trusted Lisa when she said I needed to get out of my condo and get a social life. Life could not be all about work forever.

My personal life had been on hold for years as I raised my daughter, Brooke, in California. Brooke had recently graduated from high school and, as she prepared to leave the nest, I had prepared to cautiously start dating.

I have always been the type who enjoys the rush of a fresh start. I visited California on a business trip and immediately was taken with its beauty: the old-world glamour of the Pasadena Ritz-Carlton, the brilliant sunrises bursting over the Pacific Ocean, the breathtaking, rugged terrain and, of course, the glorious weather, especially compared to what I experienced in New England. I knew I had to be a part of this place. So, when I had a chance to leave my job at 34 and start over somewhere new, Brooke and I packed up our home in Connecticut and flew to California for our new beginning.

"Don't start comparing houses," I told my daughter when we settled in Pasadena and found ourselves surrounded by extreme wealth and privilege.

Though I was a single mother, I worked hard to keep up a certain lifestyle for Brooke. She first attended an academically challenging Lutheran school, which was predominantly Korean, and later Flintridge Preparatory School, one of the top college prep schools in the state.

Like every parent, I wanted Brooke to have everything she needed, along with some of the things she wanted. But glancing around at her new friends, I knew I also would need to work to keep her expectations in check. There would be no shopping sprees on Rodeo Drive or closets overflowing with the top designer labels. Once in a while, though, I would make sure she got something from a new designer. Her classmates may have carried Chanel bags, but she had her own Coach and Juicy Couture and was allowed to borrow my Prada.

For so many years, my daughter came first, my legal practice came second, and I was lucky to be fourth or fifth on my priority list. Most of the time, I did not make the list at all.

Now, without anything keeping me in California, I was in a good place to take another leap. I took on a high-profile, contentious divorce case and flew back to the East Coast. I traveled with my assistant, Erin, and four suitcases between us to Connecticut to represent the wife of a well-known, former professional athlete.

We rented a three bedroom condo in Stamford, Connecticut, and used the first two levels of the home as a makeshift office while we lived upstairs. It was barely a shell of a home. I had pieced together secondhand office furniture to fill the rooms and make them usable. When I finally had time to watch TV, I sat on the floor in front of my little eighteen-inch set and tears would just roll down my face. I felt numb.

My client was excessively neat and hated coming to our office, but it was functional and that was all that really mattered to me. Besides, we were here to fight for her in court, not to win any awards for home design.

I was absorbed entirely in her divorce case and working practically around the clock. My hair was thinning as evidence of my exhaustion, coming out in matted fistfuls in the shower. This was the price of my late nights and stress-filled days. When I'm working on a trial, nothing else matters.

Yes, I am a divorce attorney and no, we are not immune from leading with our hearts instead of our heads when it comes to our personal relationships. When I am in my work zone, the most fun I can expect on a Friday night is busy preparations for court the next week, while *Law & Order: SVU* reruns illuminate the room from my old television set.

So it was refreshing to be out with Lisa for a change, laughing and chatting as we drove into the city. Being out in the world was hard; I felt like I was sleepwalking — socially and emotionally paralyzed — but I was going to put myself out there. Maybe I did not look or feel great, but I knew I needed to show up and meet this man, this Dennis F. Hightower.

Truly, I just wanted to feel like a human being again.

Lisa's face said it all when she saw me that night — I was tired and gaunt and barely functional. Still, when we spotted a free parking space on the street just across from the hotel, I took that as a good omen for the evening. It was going to be okay. I felt ready to step out into the springtime rain and reclaim my life.

"I know it's not exactly sexy," I thought as I smoothed out my simple monochromatic blazer and skirt. "But if he likes me, he will have to like me on a bad hair day and in plain clothes."

We met in the restaurant. I had hot tea. Lisa had a ginger ale and appetizers. And Dennis had the smile of a much younger man.

He was twenty-three years my senior and smaller in stature than anyone I had dated in the past, but he pulled out our chairs and whispered compliments as I took my seat. He smelled good; he was very well-groomed in a crisp black dress shirt and suit vest, and I soon noticed that his attentions were laser-focused on me.

"Dori, Lisa tells me you are only on the East Coast temporarily? That California is truly your home." He smiled and gestured at me with neatly clasped hands. He had such strong looking hands.

"Yes, I moved back to Connecticut for six months. I'm finishing up a demanding trial, and the six weeks pretrial prep made it necessary to be back here full time," I replied, realizing as I listened to my own voice that I had nearly forgotten how to make conversation with anyone outside the courtroom. It had been so long that just forming a sentence felt uncomfortable and foreign.

"I understand," Dennis continued, his voice filled with gentle appreciation. "I respect your dedication, but that must be hard on you, too."

"I suppose, maybe at times. My daughter is studying at NYU now, so it's comforting to be closer to her. Although I feel like with her away at school, it's also time for me to get out and rediscover my own life."

He nodded sympathetically, as if he could easily read between the lines; as if he could read me. Dennis had a certain cadence to his voice that caught my attention. He enunciated his words in a way that was so distinguished and beautiful. I just liked listening to him speak as our eyes met across the table. His dark brown eyes were so kind.

"I went through a tough divorce after forty-two years of marriage myself. You learn to be a role model for your children in different ways. It makes you stronger. Perseverance. Patience. Perception. As well as finding new ways to be present," he folded and unfolded his hands as he spoke, accenting his words with precise gestures; his voice was sure and steady.

It was not love at first sight for me, nothing quite that magical or straightforward, but he interested me. Dennis Hightower was intriguing, the way he spoke and held eye contact. He was unlike anyone I had ever met.

Lisa nodded and smiled. I was not sure if she was approving of Dennis' sentiments or of the way he was looking at me, but I followed her lead and smiled back at her.

As the night went on, Dennis told us stories about his travels around the world. His tales took us to Russia, Brazil, India and China, always setting off for luxury hotels and international business meetings. He was bold, intelligent, a force of nature and being in his company felt good.

He told us about his family compound in La Antigua, Guatemala, and his beautiful home in Washington, D.C., and he suggested we visit him in Washington sometime soon. This was my swiftly scrawled invitation into his world and his life.

We readily accepted, and Dennis beamed with delight. He had barely taken his eyes off me the entire night.

As we left the restaurant that night, emerging back out onto Manhattan's rainy streets like a scene from a movie and making our way through the crowded sidewalk to the rental car, Lisa clutched my arm and cooed, immensely pleased with herself, "Oh, I think there's going to be a wedding!" She practically did a little happy dance.

"You're crazy," I replied.

"No, I think I'll be going to a wedding."

I woke up the following morning sensing the butterflies of a new beginning. I felt alive for the first time in years, soaking in that excitement of not knowing exactly what was going to happen next.

Lisa soon phoned to tell me Dennis had emailed her after midnight.

"Oh my God, I really like her," he wrote. "What do you suggest as my next move?"

She had plenty of ideas, starting with the flowers Dennis sent me the very next day. He asked Lisa to help facilitate that second date in Washington, D.C., as soon as he returned from an upcoming board meeting in Europe.

Lisa was elated that her matchmaking was working. I knew she wanted the best for me, and she had every reason to believe Dennis F. Hightower was the best. She had already been planning a trip to Washington, D.C., with a few of her clients and asked me to join them. With that, Dennis began to plan a three-day whirlwind of a date.

He had every detail mapped out from the moment I stepped off the train. He picked me up at Union Station in his blue, classic Mercedes sports car, and he was polite as he opened the door for me and guided me into the passenger seat. I am not really a car person, but I was flattered to have someone as accomplished as Dennis trying so hard to impress me.

I was staying at the Four Seasons in Georgetown. Dennis and I wandered arm-in-arm along the brick sidewalks of pretty, historic neighborhoods before we joined the rest of Lisa's group at a beautiful restaurant, and sat before a large fireplace. We went off on our own the next night to a lovely French restaurant. He was pulling out all the stops.

I told him I loved gardens, and that one of my favorite places to visit when I lived in Pasadena had been the Huntington Gardens in San Marino, so he took me to see Washington's U.S. Botanic Garden. He ushered me around the exhibits as I lost myself in the lush, verdant warmth and soft aromas.

Dennis had served on the board of the Corcoran Gallery of Art and arranged a private tour of the Maya Lin exhibit — intricate, modern landscapes by the woman who designed the Vietnam Veterans Memorial.

Wherever we went, Dennis would touch my arm as he held the door and my back as he led me through. I was not used to so much touching and certainly not to this level of old-fashioned chivalry. I did not know men like this still existed.

He traveled around D.C. as if it were his and his alone. "Veni, vidi, vici," he often would say: I came, I saw, I conquered. Together, I felt as though we were conquering the world.

We had our first kiss as we walked back to the hotel after seeing a movie. We were walking down the street holding hands, and Dennis leaned over and kissed me. It was so natural and easy. I had worried that, being older, he would be sort of a fuddy-duddy, but he knew how to kiss. It was a perfect moment in the midst of those three bustling days.

Before I returned to Connecticut, he presented me with a small jade frog. He told me he had asked his son, Dennis Jr., to send it to him from Guatemala.

"The frog is a symbol of abundance," he said. I turned the little frog over, gently pressing it into my palm: a token of luck for our burgeoning relationship.

The Collector

Dennis was a collector. This much was clear from the moment I set foot in his home in Washington, D.C. The tidy, three-bedroom had belonged to his parents, and he now shared ownership with his younger brother, Marvin.

Marvin had done his undergraduate work at Harvard and worked as an archivist at its library. He and Dennis were not close in their younger years, but would share the house after Marvin retired.

The home was on a tree-lined street in northwest D.C., in a neighborhood nick-named the Gold Coast, a bastion of the Black Elite. For generations, well off Afri-can-American lawyers, doctors and government officials had called the Gold Coast home. It was a hub of influence and culture — one that Dennis discussed proudly at any opportunity.

The home felt like a small museum to me — everything carefully edited and dis-played with purposeful thought and care. I had never seen anything quite like it. Dennis collected African art, Russian hand-painted miniature boxes, Mexican artifacts and treasured relics from before Columbus, but his collection of Chinese jade was the featured exhibit.

I did not know a thing about jade, but I listened as he told me about it.

Like wandering the Smithsonian, everything that earned its place within Dennis' walls had a particular purpose; everything mattered, right down to the particular tint of the eggshell paint on the walls and the angle of placement for each object.

It was overwhelming. I was not sure how to walk through this house and I could not imagine living there — the objects almost seemed to compete for the oxygen in the room. Some of his collectibles had a strong vibe, a sort of power that set me on edge. I had never lived in a world where people acquired such possessions, let alone collected them on this scale.

Like a modern-day Gatsby, Dennis shuttled me from room to room, telling me proudly about his belongings and the histories of his collections. He was the cura-tor, the tour guide and the archivist in one. Standing amid his collections, Dennis looked every bit the educated, discerning and successful man he wanted me to think he was.

Among his displays, he also had memorabilia from his time at the Walt Disney Company and from his alma maters, Howard and Harvard universities. Howard blue and white and Harvard crimson appeared at every turn, as did signed posters of Simba and Ariel. It was a living résumé.

Cases displayed his medals from the United States Army; his Bronze Stars and Purple Heart lined up like little toy soldiers on a shelf. Diplomas, certificates and newspaper articles heralded his success, and trophies overflowed their cases, hoarded like a pirate's loot.

His collections, it seemed, were stories about Dennis F. Hightower, the world traveler; the educated, powerful, accomplished man. Stories about where he had been and, naturally, where he was headed — straight to the top. They were purposefully placed conversation starters, a backdrop for houseguests, friends or anyone else passing through, skillfully designed to emphasize his importance and suggest wealth, influence and power.

These were the stories Dennis told the world and the stories he told himself.

Dennis texted with Lisa the entire time I was on the train back to Connecticut. She was thrilled.

"I want this woman in my life. What should I do next?" he typed on his Blackberry.

Of course Lisa was happy to help, and they discussed possible opportunities. He wanted to know everything: "The Book of Dori," she called it. To her matchmaking eye, it was a perfect situation. For him, our relationship could be a fountain of youth, and for me, it was a chance to rediscover myself and bring some balance back into my life.

My return to reality would be short-lived. Dennis showed up at my door just before Mother's Day weekend. He had written me a letter that he titled "Ode to Dori."

"Happy Mother's Day to a Wonderful Woman — My Dream Come True," I read.

I looked up at him wondering where this was going.

"For in all the world, in any language, in any voice, in any heart, there is no one Loved as much as you…!" his letter continued.

He listed the gifts he had considered giving me — jewelry, spa vacations, gift certificates — before revealing that my gift was parked outside. He had bought me a car because he knew I did not have one on the East Coast, and he plotted with Lisa to surprise me with it that weekend.

We went outside and I could only stare, somewhat dumbstruck, at my new black 2010 Mercedes GLK.

At first I could not believe it was genuinely a gift. Were there strings attached? What was he expecting? We had known each other a matter of weeks, a time in a relationship when a bouquet of flowers would have been a lovely surprise. But a car? I was venturing into uncharted waters.

From a practical perspective, I could not deny I needed a car. So, feeling a little nervous, extremely overwhelmed and entirely grateful, I accepted his gift.

Later, I told my mother about it over the phone. "What does that mean?" I asked.

"It means he must be serious!" she replied, happy to hear someone was looking out for me and working so hard to sweep me off my feet.

Getting swept up in the storybook romance was easy. Dennis loved a grand gesture; the bigger, the better. A few days after he brought me the car, he gave me a platinum American Express card and told me it had no limit.

A part of me was screaming that it was all too much — the card, the car, the expensive meals — but what was I going to do? I was lost in Dennis' words. He was the master of his universe, the sort of person who carries a certain presence wherever he goes. What he lacked in stature — standing five feet, five inches on a good day — he more than made up for with his charm.

He had my attention.

I made it clear to Dennis during these early days that I had no intention of being his plaything, a younger girlfriend who would be at his beck and call while he was running around Washington, D.C. I was still a little gun-shy from my first marriage, and I wanted to move slowly and guard my heart in this new relationship.

When I had told Lisa I thought I was ready to start dating again, I figured I would go on a few dates over the course of the summer, see what was out there and get used to the idea of being back in the dating pool. I never could have expected to meet someone like Dennis straight away. The idea was never even on my radar.

At that point in my life, I cared more about my daughter's résumé than my dating profile.

I met my first husband at a party soon after college. We were both there with other people; we danced and, at the end of the night, I gave him my number. We dated for a little over a year and got married, but we were so young, and he was not honest with me about his past. I think he thought he was marrying someone like my mother, who would keep a stable, beautiful home.

He did not get what he was expecting and neither did I, but at least I got Brooke.

After ending the marriage, I shut the door on romance for a long time, but I had never shut the door on the dream of having more children. In my fantasy life, I pictured myself with three children. I wanted that complete picture: the happy marriage, the healthy children, the white picket fence and the little dog. I'd be lying if I said the idea of building that perfect family with Dennis had not crossed my mind. I was forty-four years old and had never experienced a real, honest-to-goodness, fairy-tale romance.

I also had never fussed much with my appearance. I appreciated style; I came of age in the '80s, and I loved beautiful, extravagant things, but I had never spent much money on myself. Instead, I found my own ways to indulge my style cravings. While I was studying at Bennington College on scholarships, I wrote papers for far wealthier students and, in exchange, they gave me their old clothes: beautiful, barely-worn pieces that I never could have bought for myself retail.

Now Lisa was going with me to see Claudette Fried, my new stylist. Lisa knew Dennis was being vetted already for a place in the Obama Administration and, if that came to pass, I would need to up my wardrobe ante for formal events we would attend together. Claudette — who had been the makeup artist to Gayle King, Oprah's best friend and co-anchor of *CBS This Morning* — knew clothes and makeup. She knew what I would need to be able to mingle with the Washington elite and ascend to a higher platform.

"You need a red dress, Dori," Lisa called to me across the room as Claudette helped me pull together a wardrobe that would be appropriate for Dennis F. Hightower's girlfriend.

Of course, Dennis was pulling all the strings.

I spent hours trying on beautiful clothes, learning which designers suited me and what would create the right image. I also was having second thoughts as I looked at the price tags. The idea of spending that much money on clothes was so overwhelming that I started tearing up in the dressing room.

"What am I doing?" I thought as I slipped a dress back onto its hanger. "I don't need any of these things!"

Finally, Lisa decided to call for backup and got Dennis on the phone.

"We're putting her in St. John," she told him.

"Perfect," Dennis replied.

"Why don't I hold off buying these things until later," I said.

"Use the card, Dori," Lisa said..

"I don't know," I replied. "Should I?"

"Yes! He gave it to you to use!" she urged as I finally, though hesitantly made my purchases.

I was using every bit of restraint in me not to put everything back and leave empty-handed, but Claudette and Lisa pushed me forward. I held my breath as I handed over my platinum Amex — Dennis' card.

I spent $10,000 in a matter of hours on my St. John wardrobe: a gown, a suit I could wear for Dennis' confirmation hearing, a jacket, two blouses and some dress pants. I was paralyzed with anxiety all the way home, worried that Dennis would think I had spent too much money, but he did not even bat an eye.

In reality, however, he was already keeping a record.

Late that spring, just five weeks into our relationship, I took a train to visit Dennis once again in Washington, D.C. He picked me up and drove me to his house. I was feeling disheveled, tired and hungry from the trip, but he sat me down in the sunroom and put on some music. As Etta James crooned softly in the background, Dennis began to speak. The way his words flowed told me he had been rehearsing for days.

"I want to spend the rest of my life with you, Dori," he began.

My face must have gone completely blank as I stared at him, the weight of his words washing over me. Was this really happening? To me?

"I never thought that I could feel like this — you are my soul mate," he said. "Will you marry me?"

I was in shock. So soon? Could he be serious? My mind scrambled for words, my thoughts racing as I sat frozen in place. What do you say when a man — this great man who has swept you off your feet, but you still hardly know — is standing before you asking you to be his wife?

He waited expectantly for an answer. I was so stunned I forgot I had not replied.

"Yes or no, Dori?" Dennis asked.

"Absolutely! Yes!" I said finally. "Yes!"

This was everything I had ever wanted, wasn't it? I loved Dennis, and even if I felt things were moving much too fast, how could I say no? Besides, I thought, we could always continue getting to know one another during a long engagement.

He presented me with a gorgeous diamond and emerald ring as a placeholder until he could choose my actual engagement ring. He had selected the emerald because he knew I loved green.

We went to dinner at Bistrot Lepic & Wine Bar in Georgetown to celebrate our engagement and, after dinner, we slept together for the first time.

"Interesting…" I thought as I noticed a mirror strategically positioned by his bed. Then I noticed his tighty-whities and thought to myself, we'll need to do something about that. Not so sexy.

I was worried about sex with someone so much older than I was, but Dennis knew what he was doing. Everything felt so natural, and he was very gentle when necessary. Not a single worry remained as I fell asleep that night, safe with Dennis, my placeholder ring twinkling in the dark. Everything seemed to be entirely perfect.

The next morning, everything was spinning — a whole new life was taking shape in a matter of hours.

I asked for a prenuptial agreement as a matter of principle. I wanted to ensure that Brooke would inherit my three-unit rental property out in California. Dennis also had two adult children and three grandchildren at the time, so I believed we would simplify our lives together by having everything cleanly spelled out for their futures. After all, I was a divorce lawyer and wanted to avoid the traps I dealt with every day.

We drove together to Westport, Connecticut, to see a prominent divorce attorney for a consultation. Seated in the luxurious office, I disclosed that, in terms of assets, I owned a small office building in California; had built a small bicoastal, legal practice; and owned a three-unit rental property in California, where Brooke and I had lived in one unit and rented the others. Otherwise, I had accumulated some debt, my credit was not great, and I did not have any real savings. I had paid for private college preparatory schools for my daughter since first grade with my parents help, and breaking even had not always been easy

Sitting beside me, Dennis stated that he was worth between $6 million and $8 million and had no debt.

After the consultation, Dennis changed his mind and said he decided he did not want a prenuptial agreement after all.

"I don't want us starting off our marriage this way," he told me. "We don't have to focus on the money."

I was hesitant. I wanted the prenup to demonstrate that I respected his family and he respected mine. Still, in the end, Dennis and I agreed to the alternative the lawyer had proposed. I had no reason to believe his plan was not fair.

Dennis met with an estate attorney and arranged that everything he had not already stipulated for his grandchildren would go to his son and to me. He also secured a $3-million life-insurance policy that I would own. Implicit in this arrangement was the understanding that I would take care of Dennis in his old age.

At that time it seemed strange to me that the party with more to lose, the one with a much higher net worth, would reject a prenup. Still, Dennis knew just what I needed to hear and convinced me he only wanted to provide for Brooke and me. He assured me that he was going to help me put my finances in order, beginning by paying off my tax debt. It was "a drop in the bucket" for him anyway, he said, so it only made sense.

Dennis also said I should stop working.

My mother was worried after I told her about Dennis' suggestion. She came from the island of Antigua. Her Scottish father was the overseer on a plantation, and her mother was a black maid. My mother moved to the Bronx at fourteen and married my father while she was still a teenager.

My parents had big dreams and were not afraid to work hard to make them happen. My mother went to Hunter College while working full time during the day. She majored in English and minored in Math and Education. She taught elementary school while my sister and I were growing up, and she believed strongly that a woman should always be able to take care of herself.

Lisa also was worried about what this would mean for me — I had worked so hard for years to get where I was in my career.

I could not hear them — my mother and my friend. I had never really had a man want to take care of me before, and I was touched that Dennis was looking out for my well-being and helping me build a better life. I decided I would go along with his wishes and lighten my workload. And, although Dennis' plan was different than the prenup I had envisioned, I accepted it and felt comfortable that my future was safe in his hands. I trusted him completely.

The Elite

Dennis' college alma mater, Howard University, is one of the most prestigious, historical black colleges in the United States. It also is a breeding ground for the Black Elite.

After attending Howard or other choice universities, the Black Elite occupy the upper tiers of business with the same sense of privilege and power as the predominantly white Old Boys' Clubs of the past. Their accomplishments fill the pages of *Black Enterprise* magazine as they ascend the corporate ladder and seek out positions on boards of the Fortune 500 and other emerging, top-notch companies.

They have built their own particular brand of upper class. The Black Elite live in the right neighborhoods; wear the right clothes and vacation in the right places — flocking to Martha's Vineyard or Paris and other "in" destinations. They belong to the Boule or to other prominent black fraternities and sororities. Some of their wives belong to The Links and the Junior League and their children, Jack & Jill, where they would make the right sort of friends.

Like their white counterparts, they are not always as concerned with bettering society so much as bettering themselves, boosting each other with phone calls and favors, recommendations and appointments.

For better or for worse, this particular group of educated African-American men and women, aligned with each other early in their social and professional lives, pledged to each other...what, exactly? For some it becomes more than a friendship; it becomes a loyalty with blurred boundaries.

I knew the Black Elite existed, but I had no idea just how all encompassing its power could be. I simply did not come from that world. My father never conformed to the ways of the Black bourgeoisie or wished to be part of the Black Elite. He made it clear that we were not a part of that.

When I was growing up in New Rochelle, my family did not belong to the social clubs or prominent black organizations. Dad was a cultural anthropologist and my parents raised my sister and me with a global perspective. A diverse education was more valuable than the accouterments of success. Our world was diverse.

Some members of the Black Elite are not just rising to the top of business and government by playing the game; they have created their own game, separate from the pack and governed by their own rules.

As I happily imagined my wedding day and showed off my glittering, five-carat engagement ring — the one Dennis had designed with a cushion-cut center stone and two sparkling side stones — I never could have guessed his games already were in play, and I was merely a pawn.

"You want to get married when?" I asked Dennis, raising an eyebrow practically off my face. I did not even attempt to hide my shocked expression.

"I want to get married as soon as possible," he repeated. "Maybe August. August 20th is my mother's birthday."

My jaw dropped. I never dreamt he would want to get married so soon and, as it turned out, during one of the busiest and most transformative months of our lives. I was already having trouble keeping pace with Dennis, who was constantly here, there and everywhere. Time was accelerating now; everything was changing and falling into position for what was to come — just as Dennis had planned. Late summer would be a time of beginnings for the Hightowers — a new marriage, a new home and for Dennis, a new role in the Obama Administration.

Dennis, my parents, Brooke and I went to Italy in July for my mother's goddaughter's wedding. It was the most beautiful ceremony at a romantic villa in Tuscany —in the town of Capalbio that boasts a beautiful medieval castle. People from all over the world traveled there for the occasion and, of course, Dennis jumped at the opportunity to see and be seen.

Sunset illuminated the Italian countryside in pink as twinkling strands of lights and the sparkle of champagne lit up the wedding celebration. I saw my parents laughing, Brooke dancing and Dennis chatting up the father of the bride. He always wanted to be in the center of the action, at the heart of everything. I had never known anyone so bright, so richly alive. I admired his certain ease in social situations; it was different from my own quiet nature.

Dennis, who now knew he would step into the role of Deputy Secretary of Commerce after we returned home, was seated in a place of respect near a colleague of the bride's father during the reception.

I had been to Italy before, but seeing it through Dennis' eyes was a new experience. He was a seasoned traveler and made me feel more secure. I watched him play camp counselor to my family as he ushered us onto the train from Rome and carefully selected our accommodations.

We had sex nonstop all around our lavish hotel room, which had a grand fresco stretching across the wall and ceiling.

Dennis took Brooke on a shopping spree. He bought her Gucci sneakers, a small Louis Vuitton bag and fabulous clothes. She had never been showered with gifts like that before; Dennis was working hard to win her over. He bought my mother a beautiful purple Furla purse and took me shopping at Escada and Roberto Cavalli.

I knew Dennis was enjoying being the big shot, and I was touched to see him trying to impress my family. He was pulling out all the stops to earn their approval. My mother puts up a lot of walls as a rule, but I could tell by the time she left Italy that she was cautiously accepting of her future son-in-law, who was only a few years younger than she.

After our time in Rome and Tuscany, Dennis and I stayed a little longer to visit Siena. He wanted to take me there because I love horses, and he wanted me to see the famous Palio races.

Each section of Siena has its own colors and banners for the parades that accompany the races. We went into a jewelry store to choose a charm showing the colors of the neighborhood of our hotel, and the girl at the counter lit up when she spotted my new handbag.

"Oh my God, that's Chanel! The spring 2009 collection!" she squealed. "So beautiful!"

"Thank you," I replied, glancing down at my little clutch. I could not believe someone would be able to identify the brand from across the room, let alone the actual collection. I smiled and took Dennis' arm as we studied the bright colors and designs, choosing one with my favorite shade of green.

We were flying high that summer and I did not know if my feet would ever touch the ground again.

CHAPTER 2

THE MAGIC MIRROR

"Sit here, Dori, for the cameras," Dennis instructed, positioning me exactly where he thought I belonged in the room.

I wondered how he could know the perfect placement. It was another new aspect to him, like he was speaking a different language.

It was August 5th, the day of Dennis' Senate confirmation hearing. I had never seen anything like it: bright lights, security and the press, all in one room. Everything was precise and planned; everything dripped with a sense of importance.

My skin crawled with a mix of anticipation and anxiety as I waited in my Dennis-approved chair. I thought he wanted me to be seen by the cameras because he was proud to have me there with him. It seemed strange, but I trusted him and did not question his intentions.

This was Dennis' day. He had told me after our second date that he was being considered for the position of Deputy Secretary of Commerce. Vernon Jordan, an advisor and so-called best friend to former President Bill Clinton, had recommended him for the position.

We had been planning to go to Amsterdam that summer, but Dennis had to change our plans and stay home to complete the lengthy application process. I knew this was important, but I had no idea what it meant for him and for us. Everything was changing.

My parents came with me to Washington, D.C. It was my official debut as Dennis' fiancée, and everything had to be perfect. I had chosen my shoes, a lower pair of brown Dolce and Gabbana heels, so I would not be taller than Dennis in photos.

Dennis loved to shop for me and dress me up. He cared about style and was knowledgeable about top designers. St. John was a favorite of his because it was upscale and I could have the pieces tailored so they were not matronly or too conservative. To him, St. John meant class. He knew the precise look he wanted for his fiancée, and he knew how to channel wealth through a wardrobe.

Dressing for photo ops was an art form, one that was still entirely foreign to me. I had been living out of suitcases when we met, scrambling to pull together an outfit suitable for an ordinary day in court. Dennis' world was never ordinary, and dressing for it involved a great deal more stress.

I used to shop at discount stores and searched the racks for bargains, but Dennis would have none of that. Now I wore what Claudette selected for me, slowly learning to choose clothes without worrying about the price tag.

For the confirmation hearing, I was Dennis' Jackie O in a soft, mint green St. John suit, my hair styled to hide the thinning spots that were just now beginning to fill back in.

I had to be taught how to put on makeup. Until I met Dennis, I had worn only a minimal amount: a dab of concealer and swipe of lip balm — never a full face. I also had to learn to do more with my hair than pull it up in a ponytail or bun.

Before I was plunged into the world of makeup artists and stylists, I was mostly oblivious to the amount of work that goes on behind the scenes to create even the most seemingly casual appearance — the precision and the planning. No one rolls out of bed looking like Michelle Obama. That look of success and polish takes a whole team.

I began to appreciate in a new way how in many cases political wives subjugate much of their personalities and give up a great deal to make their husbands the star of the show.

Polished in my designer suit and perfect makeup, I glanced around the room before the hearing began, checking in with the familiar faces for reassurance. I exchanged a glance with my mother and shot Dennis a supportive smile.

"I can do this," I thought to myself. This is what all the ballet lessons, horseback riding camps and sacrifices my parents made to expose me to culture were all about. My head was already pounding and the room was abuzz with activity, but everything melted away when Dennis began to speak.

I would like to introduce the Members of the Committee to my son, Dennis F. High-

tower, Jr.; my fiancée, Dori Bye, and her parents, Mr. and Mrs. Melvin Bye; my cousins, other relatives, close friends and business colleagues, many of whom have traveled great distances to support me today.

— Opening Remarks by Dennis F. Hightower at his Senate confirmation hearing

It sounds silly, but I loved watching Dennis prepare for his speeches. He had a wonderful speaking voice and could go on at length on any subject. I would just sit and listen as he practiced, writing and rewriting, reading the words aloud, playing with emphasis and tone. When he spoke, he was charming in every way — the sort of person who made you want to sit up and pay attention.

I had never seen anyone who functioned at such a high level — going over his words for hours until everything was exactly right. He saved copies of nearly every speech he had ever written.

Wish Upon A Star

Hope.

It was the word on the tip of everyone's tongue as Obama took office. This administration would be different: idealistic, honest and fair. Maybe as African-Americans, we considered ourselves greater in some way for our history, more concerned with equality and for the well-being of every citizen.

Some of us were naïve.

Great intentions do not necessarily pan out. From the very start, the wolves were circling, looking to gain access to power.

Perhaps it was a sign that African-Americans truly had arrived. Some of those in power were playing the same games and doing so with the same total abandon as their white predecessors.

Becoming wrapped up in Dennis' power was so easy. Standing beside this seemingly great man, I felt I finally could offer Brooke access to a global lifestyle few experienced; she would even get to meet the President and First Lady. It was nothing short of a fairy tale. I could bring my mother to the White House at Christmastime to see the glittering lights and gorgeous displays, and see her beaming with pride. And I could sit here, just watching Dennis' face and feel a warm contentment just to have his love and respect, honored to be his fiancée and sitting together on the verge of something truly special.

As I look at the challenges facing America and the Department of Commerce, I am reminded of a saying that defined the mission of one of the elite fighting forces I was a member of, and that is: "Rangers lead the way."

Dennis studied acting and elocution because he knew it would help him get ahead in business. He read. He studied. He told me he spoke Russian, Spanish and French in addition to English. My contemporaries come from the hip-hop generation; there just are not many of us who are as well read as Dennis, I thought.

I was starting to understand what Lisa knew when she thought to introduce us. I think she hoped that if the relationship worked out, she could add celebrity matchmaker to her résumé, but she also knew I often felt like an old soul, much more serious than many of my peers, so an older man might be a better match.

"You'll grow from this, Dori," she had told me. "It'll be good for you."

"Maybe you're right," I said. Certainly relationships with men my age had not worked out in the past.

Today, the Department of Commerce must lead the way to improved economic growth, enhanced job creation and a future that is brighter than our past.

As I posed for the cameras, not a single hair out of place, I felt as though this was just the beginning of our story, our fairy tale. At Dennis' side, smiling blind into the flashing lights, our future seemed bright too.

CHAPTER 3

SLEEPING BEAUTY'S CASTLE

August seemed like it would never end. We were rushing from place to place — planning the wedding in between all the functions and formalities of Dennis' new job. Looking back, it's truly a wonder we made it to our wedding day at all.

I did not want a big, elaborate wedding or anything resembling a white wedding gown. I had fallen in love with an exquisite gorgeous Brioni dress I saw in an Italian magazine. I mentioned to Dennis that it was exactly what I was looking for, nothing like a traditional bridal look.

Once we returned home from Tuscany, Dennis surprised me yet again by tracking down that same dress in New York City for our wedding. He wore a crisp white linen suit and presented me with a dazzling diamond bracelet that glittered brightly in the summer sun.

On his mother's birthday, August 20, we gathered a dozen of our closest family and friends for a simple and elegant ceremony at the Delamar Hotel in Greenwich, Connecticut. The Presidential Suite looked out over the harbor filled with yachts and the Justice of the Peace married us in a ceremony that was sweet and heartfelt.

My 'something borrowed' was a small paddle with a piece of scripture written on it. I found it abandoned in a ladies room when Dennis and I had visited the Harvard Club in New York City earlier that summer. The Club was a world unto itself. A structure I frequently walked past in New York. From the outside one couldn't possibly grasp the scale. The neo-Georgian style architecture and enormous fireplace were regal in every sense.

The paddle must have been left behind from a wedding at the club. I do not know why it caught my attention the way it did, but I took it with me to read during our wedding.

And I will betroth thee unto me forever; yea, I will betroth thee unto me in righteousness, and in judgment, and in loving kindness, and in mercies. I will even betroth thee unto me in faithfulness: and thou shalt know the Lord –Hosea 2:19-20

Even though our children were adults, we wanted them to know they were now part of our new family too. We gave Dennis Jr. and Brooke artwork as gifts to symbolize the joining of our families. My parents and sister were there, along with Dennis' brother, Marvin, his long-time housekeeper, Maria, and, of course, Lisa, who had predicted our wedding from the very start, though she never could have guessed just how quickly her prediction would come true. We all posed for pictures together after the ceremony, laughing and smiling as Greenwich Harbor glistened crystal blue in the background.

The days surrounding our wedding were nothing short of magical. I went to bed happy and woke up happy in my new life as Mrs. Dennis F. Hightower.

I loved the photos we took that day, but I never assembled my wedding album. The pictures remained in jumbled stacks, filling envelopes and shoeboxes. I would never have the leisure to be sentimental. I would never sit in the evening and run a finger across a wedding photo, thinking wistfully over the details of our ceremony. In the whirlwind days and months that followed, there would never be enough time for nostalgia.

Dennis and I closed on our new home the day after we married.

It was called Fleur D'Eau, a name that conjured images of a storied place tucked deep in the countryside of Provence. The home itself was a fortress built of whitewashed bricks with a slate tile roof. Moated by water flowing down to the backyard pond and river, it peered down on neighboring homes from its hilltop perch, up a long and winding drive.

We were house hunting for several weeks before finding Fleur D'Eau. In fact, Dennis initially put in an offer for a much more expensive home that was newly built. It was on Davis Road in prestigious Greenwich and would have run close to $6 million.

I told Dennis I did not need or want to live on an estate of that magnitude, and we could be comfortable in a home one-sixth of that price, but he would not hear of it. He said he would not be comfortable on an estate that was not at this level. His standards were set in stone, so we made a formal offer on the Greenwich estate, and when the bid was not accepted, we expanded our search into neighboring Stamford.

Fleur D'Eau was our compromise: a striking, $3,562,000 estate with a dozen spacious, meticulously maintained rooms and eleven bathrooms. The living spaces were nothing short of grand — the previous owners had completed a spectacular renovation, featuring a deluxe gourmet kitchen, a lavish master suite with several adjoining rooms, living quarters for housekeepers and the most complicated automated lighting scheme I had ever seen. I worried I would never learn how it all worked.

The house was at once magnificent and monstrous compared to my bungalow in California. I did not know if it would truly feel like a home to me, if I would ever get used to its rooms that went on forever and its sprawling, echoing nature. What made me love Fleur D'Eau, however, was the land. From the limestone terrace, I could look down across the beautiful property, tranquil and green and perfect in every way.

While I initially was overwhelmed by the thought of seven acres and the sheer time and expense that would be involved in its maintenance, the beauty of the grounds was alluring. I could hear owls overhead at night. Geese and herons clustered about the pond, which was alive with twenty-four species of fish.

I loved being surrounded by the wildlife that also called our acreage home. The house may have belonged to us, but the grounds were theirs alone. On any given day, I could watch herds of deer and rabbit families racing across the grassy hillside. The yard was landscaped with a variety of plantings that bloomed all year long. Just the variety of trees was impressive — silver birch, oak, evergreens and elm — the property was constantly changing and alive.

It was as pristine as it was wild. And sitting in my kitchen window seat looking out over our dominion, it was nothing short of entrancing.

Dennis and I initially agreed that ownership of Fleur D'Eau would be in both our names. He only changed his tune after our offer on the estate was accepted.

"Upon second thought, it should be in a trust," he said. "Yes, a trust."

He explained his reasoning, and I understood where he was coming from, but something still did not sit right with me. I called Lisa for advice.

"No way! That house is in your name too or you walk away," she said. "He probably will never love you more than he does right this second. He doesn't want to lose you, so trust your gut."

I knew Lisa was right, of course. So although I did not want to confront Dennis over finances so early in our relationship, I told him I was not comfortable with the estate being put into a trust. He conceded and both our names went on the title.

And with that, the house became ours, his and hers equally.

Fleur D'Eau

The name had come with the property and I never thought much about it. Like Daphne du Maurier's Manderley or Margaret Mitchell's Tara, my new home took up so much space that she seemed to require a name of her own.

I was at once caught up in her beauty and overwhelmed by her never-ending demands.

Fleur D'Eau. Flower of water, in literal French translation. A pretty little image, but it did not mean a lot. In reality it should have been called "just above water." Fitting for a home poised over a pond, and for us.

We were treading water above the world. Only sometimes, I did not know whether I was floating or drowning.

My world was spinning as we moved into Fleur D'Eau and began our life together. Dennis' time was always divided, leaving Connecticut around five in the morning on Mondays and returning from Washington late Friday evenings. He was coming and going at a frenzied pace, a speed associated with superheroes, but somehow he made it all look easy.

He stayed in touch constantly during the week, texting and calling upward of eight times each day. He was always checking in with me, professing his love time and again as he moved through his workday.

Dennis had brought his housekeeper, Maria, with him. She had been with his family for ten years and followed him after his divorce from his first wife. She was a lovely, black, Dominican woman who had been working on estates since childhood. She was now 56 and in poor health from a difficult life.

Dennis was hard on Maria — military in the way he expected his home to be run. By this time, she knew his likes and dislikes and understood how to accommodate his every whim. She cared for the home accordingly, right down to ironing the sheets.

Maria would sip thick Dominican coffee, filling the kitchen with its rich aroma as she stirred a pot on the stove. Everything she cooked was delicious, while I have never been much of a cook. My mother teased me that she'd tried to teach me to cook without success, so having Maria under our roof, preparing the most beautiful meals, was an unexpected plus.

I had never had a live-in housekeeper before. At first, I worried that Maria would dislike me. She had lived with Dennis and his first wife, after all. Would she always be quietly comparing me to her? Did she trust me? Would having another person in our home all the time be intrusive?

Maria's kindness and sincerity quickly put my fears to rest. She was the type of person who lived to take care of people — traveling with us to California and maintaining relationships with Dennis' children and grandchildren even when he could not.

I had yet to learn any of the details, but I understood that Dennis had become estranged from his daughter and her family in the fallout from his first divorce.

Fleur D'Eau was large, and people were constantly coming and going. Having Maria there when Dennis was away during the week was reassuring. She kept me company, telling me stories about her family — her husband was ill back in the Dominican Republic, and she sent money home often to pay for his care.

Dennis wanted everything in the house to be immaculate, and maintaining a property of that scale was a 24/7 chore. Maria was constantly busy, and I was relieved to have her expertise. I never could have sustained his standards on my own.

Everything in Dennis' world had to be done up to the nines — an extraordinary production. And our next production would be filling this grand and largely empty home with furniture and hopefully children.

I never had the money to accumulate designer furniture. I read *Veranda* and *Architectural Digest* and loved looking at photos of beautiful rooms, but my own homes were not professionally decorated. I saved up for furniture from Domain and shopped at Pier One and The Bombay Company, buying pieces I loved and keeping them for years, or as long as they lasted.

Dennis and I had brought some furniture from our previous homes, but a cobbled-together design would not be right for Dennis. He wanted every detail to be perfect.

"What's our budget for this?" I asked him one night as I sat propped up in bed, paging through a stack of magazines, beginning to compare prices and come up with plans.

"I don't know— $250,000?" he replied quickly, in a tone that told me the sky was the limit. Dennis F. Hightower did not know the word budget.

We hired a professional decorator. I remembered a couch I had seen in the pages of Veranda years earlier. It was in a photo spread, the kind of thing you skim for inspiration. I had never actually eyed a magazine spread and then looked up the designer and price of a piece. Dennis had a different approach, however. Not only did he track down the West Coast designer whose furniture was featured in the issue I saw, we flew out to California to meet her and choose our fabrics so she could make us a custom couch.

There was a small room off our master bedroom filled with another collection of Dennis' Buddhist artifacts. It was supposed to be an office, but we agreed we did not need another office. What we needed was a sex room.

In an attempt to be a bit more demure, I referred to it as the "Relaxation Room."

Soon the Relaxation Room had a mattress. It was the perfect hideaway from the world. Dennis was experienced in the bedroom; he opened me up to new things and I like to think that I had given him a new lease on life.

On our first Christmas at Fleur D'Eau, we still did not have much in the way of furniture, but we had a Christmas tree decorated entirely from Bergdorf Goodman. I cuddled up with my dog, Moe, on the floor and watched the tree sparkling, reflecting in the window as a deep chill settled over the property and the animals outside tucked themselves into burrows and dens for the winter.

Dennis showered me with gifts as he always did — greeting cards from Papyrus and lengthy, handwritten notes and typed letters positively dripping with sentiment. It was as if he constantly strived to top his own words.

"I absolutely adore you," they read. "A profound love."

Despite a rigorous schedule that split Dennis' time between Washington, D.C., Stamford and other cities, I honestly believed we were happy. And although he later held a different opinion, I never felt that Dennis wanted me to move to D.C. That was where he grew up and returned to with his first wife after he retired from Disney. It was in the past for him, and I believed him when he told me he wanted his new home — our home — to be in Connecticut, at beautiful Fleur D'Eau, far away from the looming monuments and rushing streets of Washington.

CHAPTER 4

THE PUMPKIN COACH

I was twirling and whirling now.

I could feel myself losing my grounding and my sense of self. To go from being a single mom accustomed to sitting in the driver's seat of my personal and professional life, to being entirely dependent on someone else to set my life's agenda and choose the direction…it was unsettling. I never had to follow someone else's lead in everything I did. If I was adrift when I met Dennis, now I was marooned on a distant island.

Still, there was beauty. We traveled and entertained and mingled with the Washington elite. Dennis took me into New York City to see the Alvin Ailey American Dance Theater, and we went to all his favorite restaurants and other places he deemed special.

We went shopping in Boston and he bought me a beautiful Pucci dress, a sexy Diane von Fürstenberg wrap dress and a lovely Roberto Cavalli black cocktail dress. The extravagance was still a whole new experience to me, filling my closet with luxury pieces without worrying over the price tags.

I think Dennis enjoyed shopping for me because it made him feel important, but he also knew I needed the wardrobe for all the prominent events we attended. Once, while we were at opening night of the National Symphony Orchestra at the Kennedy Center in Washington, I met another woman wearing the same St. John, one-shoulder, red gown. We laughed and took a picture together. Looking back I wonder if she had picked hers out herself.

Dennis always seemed to read my thoughts. He was constantly predicting what I needed, what I liked, what I would appreciate and value. Though he left me feeling dizzied and overwhelmed at times, he also made me feel cared for and loved.

In retrospect, it's so obvious that Lisa was still feeding him information and helping him strategize.

In preparation for a trip to Austria, Dennis took me to Albe Furs in Greenwich to purchase a new coat. He had chosen a floor length mink that he thought would look particularly elegant with my gown.

"You should get two," he said as I tried on the mink.

"Absolutely not; one is more than enough," I replied.

I liked the one he had selected, and I did not want to spend $28,000 on furs — that was ridiculous. I reminded him again that I had an old fur buried deep in my closet that would do fine for Austria, but he quickly shook his head. I do not know whether he did not like my coat or he just did not like for me to wear things I owned before we met.

Maybe he did not want me wearing anything that he had not given me. He wanted me dressed head to toe in Dennis.

We stayed in Vienna for New Year's Eve at the glamorous Hotel Sacher, a regal fortress, five-star hotel built in 1876 and famous for its decadent Sachertorte chocolate cake.

Dennis arranged for a horse-drawn carriage to take us to the Vienna Symphony and Ball one night. I wore a green gown from Neiman Marcus — fitted, classy, but not overly sexy. As we pulled away from the hotel, Dennis leaned close to point out the home of Antonio Vivaldi. I looked out from the carriage over the frosty city; it was like a scene from a snow globe, an icy world come to life just for us.

"This cannot be real," I thought to myself, breathing in Vienna's night air and all its hypnotic beauty. "I don't go to balls in Vienna. This is not my life."

I half expected the carriage to turn back into a pumpkin at any second.

I traveled very differently during the time before Dennis. I took Brooke on a flurried, four-day trip to France the year she turned sixteen. Who decides they can see all of Paris in four days? We did not care; we tackled the city like a true pair of tourists with a list of places we had to see. We had a wonderful time checking off our list, posing in front of the Eiffel Tower and taking in other sights. I wanted Brooke to have the experience of traveling in Europe, of course, but I had a secondary motivation. I wanted her to have something to talk about with her peers, for many of whom international travel was a much more frequent event.

By that time, Brooke knew the ins and outs of wealth much better than I did, thanks to her private school classmates. Brooke noticed Dennis had an American Express Centurion or "Black Card." She knew some celebrities had them, but Brooke had to explain just what it was to me.

For every fantastic adventure with Dennis, there was an equal measure of mind-numbing anxiety. I could feel it begin to creep in before any of these big events, especially functions in Washington where I knew I would be subject to posed photo ops and formal introductions.

I was not used to hunting down designer clothes or worrying about getting my hair done just right, my makeup crafted to Dennis' specifications. I was used to being Dori Bye. Now I was Dori B. Hightower, and that name carried a different weight in these circles. At times I felt like I needed an act of Congress to get to these events in a state that would suit him.

I was in my forties, and this was not the way I was used to living. I was, and always had been, a worker bee. I knew how to get things accomplished and talk shop, but now I was living in a world where my professional skills were of little-to-no use. Even so, I did not want to let Dennis down.

Throughout my career, I would remind myself time and again of the importance of showing up. So though there were nights I would rather be curled up at home with a book, I would tell myself to go to events and talk to people. There usually were few African-Americans at these functions, and that very fact added to my anxiety on many levels. However, it also reinforced for me the importance of being present — for there to be another professional black woman in the crowd.

Now, attending events with Dennis, I had to learn an entirely new skill set. Being present was not enough; I had to know how to position myself for the camera, how to be chic and poised. Nothing less would do.

Small talk was another struggle. I do not do chitchat very well, and sometimes I was simply too honest. I would ask perfectly coiffed political wives, "What do you do all day?"

They often would reply with a blank stare.

It was probably an inappropriate question, and I'm sure it came off as judgmental, but I was serious. I genuinely wanted to know how they spent their days, hour-by-hour, minute-by-minute. If they told me, maybe I finally would catch on and learn what I should be doing.

They could have told me early on, for example, that the job of political spouses is to help their partners climb. I was that naïve — I honestly could not get it through my head that I was there only to play the part of Best Supporting Wife.

"I always feel alone when I go to these events, Dori," Dennis had said once with a dramatic sigh. "I need you there with me."

"You look like you are doing fine," I said.

And he was. He was experienced and charming; he could put on the mask and work the room at a moment's notice. It never seemed to wear him out. That same atmosphere exhausted me. I'm sure his first wife was much better at it than I ever could be.

My job was to make him look good, be attractive and charismatic and never put a single, well-heeled Prada foot wrong. It was a balancing act. He did not like me to go off on my own too much at parties and suddenly became jealous if I took too much of the attention from him. I often would catch him watching me from across the room, evaluating my appearance and making note of who was talking to me and how close they were standing. He would watch my every move to make sure I stayed within the boundaries. He wanted the young pretty wife, but he did not want the attention on me. He wanted it all for himself.

I look at photos from those days and I see myself in the background, standing behind Dennis.

Lost, but still smiling — blind.

Dennis and I had discussed children early in our relationship. Having another baby was never a question for me. I would not have married him if he had said he did not want children. Why get married if not to have a family?

"Would you ever want to have a baby?" I had asked him plainly.

"Yes," Dennis replied. "I'm so flattered you would want to have a baby with me."

In retrospect, he was probably only telling me what he thought I wanted to hear.

I thought a baby was part of our plan and I believed we were on the same page. Dennis told me before we were married that he had a radical prostatectomy following his sojourn with prostate cancer, but we could still conceive through IVF.

We planned to start fertility treatments the following winter. If it did not work, I would have loved to adopt a child.

I married my first husband at twenty-two, and I was in law school when I had Brooke. It was not an easy pregnancy, but I managed to make it to graduation, just eleven days before she was born.

It had been only the two of us since she was six years old. We had lived in a classic New England colonial by the water at St. Mary's by the Sea in Bridgeport, Connecticut, before moving out to sunny Pasadena. Brooke was my whole world. Now that I was suddenly remarried, I wanted more than anything to have another child.

I knew the odds were not in our favor right from the start, but with a bit of faith, some luck and a lot of money, I fully believed we would get our baby.

In January 2010, we began fertility treatments. I was forty-five years old and had to start by giving myself daily injections of clomid. Dennis' prostatectomy had left him unable to ejaculate. He would need a surgical procedure in which doctors would go in to harvest his sperm.

Even before we married, Dennis took me to see his urologist in Washington, and they referred us to a fertility doctor in the same medical complex. I was willing to go along with his choice, but the logistics of fertility treatments in Washington while living in Connecticut were a nightmare. We rented an apartment for a few weeks during my treatments so I could be close to the doctor's office.

The injections made me feel terrible — nauseous and bloated from the hormones. I saw an acupuncturist during the process. It was miserable, but I intended to do whatever it took to get pregnant.

I was still handling some lingering court cases in Connecticut, and the logistics were growing more and more challenging from Washington.

Dennis suggested I close down what remained of my legal practice and focus on getting pregnant. This time I conceded and made plans to stop working altogether.

"Why don't you go to a fertility doctor in New York and get a second opinion?" Lisa asked when I told her about the situation. "Don't close your practice! You don't want to be a woman without your own means. And what am I going to tell your clients?"

"I have already done it," I replied, "and the Washington doctor is who Dennis wants me to see. It will be fine."

I could tell she was suspicious of Dennis' intentions, like he was somehow stacking the deck and playing games by sending me to the doctor he chose in Washington, but I just could not see it. Besides, I did not care where I went to see a doctor, as long as we could have a baby.

As I lay in bed in the apartment, I thought back over our initial consultation with the fertility doctor. Dennis and I sat together in the cold office, and Dennis listened intently as I listed off my medical history. It was not all pretty: I had a miscarriage during my first marriage, and I had abortions at times in my life when I was not ready to have children.

I rarely talked about this and it was hard to talk about it that day. I was twenty-five when I had Brooke and I always knew I wanted more children someday, but at age thirty-three I was already divorced and a single mother and I was not in a place where I could add another child to the mix. Ultimately, I made very difficult and personal decisions that many women are forced to make during their child bearing years.

Dennis was stoic. He did not say a word at the time, but he stored the information away. Later he would pull it out, saying that learning about my medical history that day changed the way he thought about me.

I sometimes forgot that Dennis was from a different generation and had a different mindset. I had reasons for every decision I had made earlier in my life, and for most of my peers this was all they needed to know. For Dennis, these choices were unacceptable.

Was that some sort of tipping point for him? The moment I became flawed in his eyes, less than perfect and therefore less worthy of his love and respect?

Apparently so.

I will never know for sure, but of all the careless and hurtful things Dennis said during his deposition when our marriage unraveled, that was somehow the comment that cut the deepest.

I wanted that chance to be a mother again and finally, I thought everything was in place. I wanted to raise another child and I wanted to do it with Dennis. I could already picture him attending father/daughter dances, the four of us going places as a family, and doing all of the things that I had missed out on with Brooke. That was my dream and it did not have anything to do with living in a fancy house or wearing designer clothes.

After one unsuccessful round of IVF, Dennis told me, seemingly out of the blue, that he did not want to try again. It was devastating to see him give up on my dream so quickly. I thought it had been our dream, something we both wanted from the start. He never gave me any reason to doubt that. If Dennis had told me he did not want children, I probably would not have married him.

Rapunzel, Rapunzel

While I was staying in Washington with Dennis, we were invited to a reception for Lisa Jackson, Administrator of the Environmental Protection Agency and the first African-American to hold the position. There was so much excitement around each new appointee at that time; so much hope for African-Americans in government.

I had to get my hair done for the event. I mentioned it to Dennis, and he recommended I go to a specific salon. I assumed one of his friends' wives had recommended the stylist. After all, Dennis liked to keep up with the latest hot spots.

He even called the salon and made the appointment for me.

Soon I was sitting in the salon chair, watching my reflection in the mirror, the reflection of a woman who was becoming more unrecognizable by the day. It had nothing to do with my hair — it was everything about my overall reflection. My expressions had changed somehow, both tense and vapid at the same time, lacking the spark of energy that used to run through even my most frenzied days.

I sighed and turned my attention to the stylist.

"How are you today, Mrs. Hightower?" he asked, landing on my name with a certain curious tone.

"I am well, thank you," I replied simply. "How are you?"

I watched his eyes in the mirror, feeling suddenly a little uneasy. The stylist worked quietly as he pursed his lips and stifled his expressions. He was clearly uncomfortable with our small talk.

"You do know," he began with a cautious and knowing look, "I did Dawn's hair for her wedding, and Denia Hightower is in here every week?"

I was mortified. Of all the top salons in Washington, D.C., Dennis had sent me straight into the firestorm smoldering around his daughter and first wife without any warning.

"Make sure you know who your friends are in Washington," the stylist added with a sort of half smile. "You don't want to trust the wrong person."

I did not know what to say. I was incredulous, fidgeting with my hands, but trying to remain composed.

"Now, what are we going to do here," he mused. "I want you to have sexy hair." I could not wait to get out of that salon.

I was in the crying-angry they messed up my hair place when Dennis picked me up. I held myself together long enough to get in the car.

"How did it go?" he asked.

"Not well. My hair is a disaster," I said. "Dennis, does your first wife go here? Does your daughter Dawn go here?"

"Yes," he shrugged. "I didn't think it would be a big deal."

I nearly choked on those words. I tried to think of a reason he would purposefully send me into that situation without warning me in advance. What if I had run into Denia Hightower or Dawn that day? Was he trying to embarrass me or play games with his ex-wife or daughter?

Was this a scheme to mess with all of us? Dennis knew it would get back to his ex-wife and daughter that I was there.

I did not even like what the stylist had done with my hair. I did not want or need "sexy hair." I had just wanted it to look nice, and now it was a freakin' "sexy" mess.

I watched Dennis' calm expression as we drove back to the Mandarin Oriental Hotel. He did not understand my concern. He simply did not hear me, so I did not speak of it again.

"It's interesting," George Robert Fuller said as we stood waiting for Dennis one morning. George is a celebrity hairdresser who has styled many big names over the course of his career including Patty LaBelle, Natalie Cole and Chaka Khan.

"What is?" I asked.

"Dennis is the first black man I've met who shows up already done."

It was true. Dennis always arrived at the breakfast table with his hair combed, nails filed, bathrobe perfectly smoothed, sash tied, everything clean and neat. He had his presentation down to a science; regardless the time of day, everything had to be in order.

Dennis had to feel in control. This was the primary trait that spanned his entire life. I commented once to his brother, Marvin, that Dennis seemed to have everything so under control. "No, Dori, he really does not," Marvin replied, dismissing my words quickly enough to let me know that he had given this a lot of thought in the past. "He looks like he has it all together, but he is not a details person."

Marvin was right. Dennis knew the big picture; his life was painted in wide brush-strokes, bright and richly saturated. Yet he could only focus on so much at one time. What Marvin had already pinpointed was that Dennis simply did not have the emotional wherewithal to zero in on the details of his picture. He could offer up the big ideas, the broad story, but he could not always support it. It was in the nitty-gritty that Dennis began to falter and lose control.

He could easily become controlling and obsessive about his appearance, too. Dennis would go through periods of very limited eating, followed by swings in the opposite direction, when he would gain a large amount of weight quickly.

When I met Dennis, he seemed to be of an average fitness level. He was in good shape for his age, but nothing exceptional. Three weeks later, he had gotten buff. After we were married, he allowed himself to fall out of shape again. His muscles atrophied and I noticed he was often out of breath on the stairs.

There was no middle ground for Dennis, physically and mentally. It was one extreme after another, and keeping up with him wore me out.

Hearing Voices

Lisa asked me to stop talking to Dennis about things we discussed.

Dennis asked me to stop talking to Lisa entirely. She was being pushed out for months and she knew it. There was room for only one voice in my head. Lisa and Dennis both had powerful voices, and he did not intend to compete.

My head was full of loud voices, and none of them were my own.

And soon, I was left with only one voice, and it belonged to Dennis.

CHAPTER 5

TREMORS

Dennis was in a meeting in his Washington, D.C. office when the pain began. He had problems with painful kidney stones for years, but this time there were complications. Twenty-four hours later, he was facing a septic infection that I later learned is fatal in one in five patients.

I had just returned to Connecticut from visiting him in Washington and quickly hurried back to be at his bedside. Dennis spent a week squirreled away at George Washington University Hospital under the name Alexandre Dumas — the author of *The Three Musketeers*. No one could know that a member of the administration was so sick.

It was April 2010, the beginning of spring. Dennis faded in and out of consciousness the first few days. His words, when he could speak, did not make a lot of sense. I could not always understand him, and I knew he was struggling. I sat by his side during the day and slept on the little couch in his private hospital room night after night.

As I lay awake one night in the hospital, listening to the insistent hum of Dennis' monitors and watching his face as he breathed in and out in a shallow, erratic pattern, I realized that for the very first time in the year that I had known him, Dennis looked every last bit his age. He was vulnerable now, this great man without a chink in his armor. This was Dennis without the bells and whistles. You cannot maintain your persona when you are feeling that weak. You are forced to be real.

It soon became clear that I was facing the very real possibility of losing him. I held my breath as I waited for updates from the doctors, taking it day-by-day and sometimes minute-by-minute. I couldn't allow myself to think about the possibility that our life together could be cut so brutally short. I sighed deeply, trying to push that fear from my brain, the sterile smell of hospital antiseptic filling my lungs.

I reached out to his children. Directly to Dennis, Jr., a.k.a. Denny, who was living in Paris at the time and asked him to speak to his sister Dawn. A volcano that erupted in Iceland forced many European countries to shut down air travel temporarily. As a result, he could not get back to the United States.

Dawn did not come either and refused to allow the grandchildren to visit.

This was the first time I began to realize just how complicated Dennis' relationship with his children was. This was not from a simple disagreement or bitterness that would ease over the years if his daughter refused to see her father on his potential deathbed. I finally understood that there was little hope of reconciliation, especially with his estranged daughter.

Even with all that was going on, Dennis still worried about outward appearances. While we were in the hospital, he found a photo of himself on Lisa's website. He asked me to call her and have her take it down immediately.

"Dennis is doing a little better but he was wondering why you posted the photo of him from the wedding," I told Lisa, pacing the edge of the hospital waiting room. "He is not happy with it."

"He is Googling himself? He's at death's door and he wants me to remove a photo?" Lisa screamed.

"Just take it down, Lisa," I requested flatly.

Dennis knew Lisa loved to talk. He would Google himself frequently and monitor mentions on social media presence, compulsively guarding his name, furious if he thought too much information was getting out. He knew the steps to take to push negative information down.

While Dennis was worrying about his social media presence, I was busy worrying about him. I started looking over his medical records and quickly learned he had some health issues, much worse than I had known. I hated being angry with him, but I was frustrated and disappointed that he had not told me about the state of his health and pre-existing conditions. I could not mention my upset to him, at least not yet. I just could not go there while he was so incredibly sick. I kept quiet as I sat on the small couch.

I knew from the start that part of being with Dennis would include caring for him as he aged; "in sickness and in health" carries more weight when one partner is significantly older than the other. I was prepared for all of this, but I needed to know what we were up against.

After a week of living in constant fear, we learned that the antibiotics had begun to take effect, and Dennis' condition began to improve. He was going to be okay. Finally, we were signing page after page of discharge forms and discussing plans for his care at home.

I knew Dennis would have to make some serious choices about his career. He had been flying all over the world, wearing himself out with conferences and speaking engagements and high-pressure meetings, all the while knowing it was taking a toll on his body.

Dennis and I returned to his Washington, D.C. home armed with a catheter and a bulk pack of adult diapers, with orders that he continue to rest. He had only been in Obama's administration for six months, but he told me that he wanted out.

People he respected in the business world were frank with him. They told him that leaving the administration after such a short tenure would not look good for him. According to Dennis, he was granted some time off to recuperate and would be able to resume his work on a more relaxed schedule. At least, that was the story Dennis told me.

His time at home would be short. Dennis, Jr. was getting married in Guatemala in May and Dennis was determined that we would attend, septic infection be damned.

Within weeks, I was standing above a toilet in Dennis' compound in Guatemala, sticky from the tropical heat and humidity trapped in the bathroom. Plastic scrub brush in hand, I went to work. The bathroom was dirty, Dennis' room was dusty, and the whole compound felt wrong to me. With Dennis' infection and the freshly bleached hospital room still fresh in my mind, I worried the sanitary conditions in this place could be unsafe for him.

Cleaning did not demand much from my mind, which soon began to wander over what I had seen since my arrival.

This was Guatemala? This was the compound, the home that Dennis had described to me from the day we met? He was always talking it up and longing to bring me for a visit. This was it? After all the five-star hotels we had stayed in, "the compound" was nothing like I had expected.

The weight of culture shock pressed on my aching head.

Dennis Jr. had met us at the airport in his BMW SUV. Guatemala was rough from the start. Though there were some undeniably beautiful vistas, the city was raw; stray dogs and armed guards with rifles walked the streets.

Dennis had warned me about the armed guards, but he said the compound was near a police station and relatively safe. Many CIA operatives retired to this region, he said, and a person could live well in Guatemala without a lot of money. Still, traveling in this area of the world was not without danger, and people had to be careful.

We passed a little gatehouse and an armed guard as we arrived at the compound. From the way Dennis had raved about the property, I had pictured the Kennedy compound in Hyannis. Instead I saw a modest one-story home behind concrete walls. Still, I tried to remain optimistic. Maybe it would be better on the inside.

I became more and more confused as I walked from room to room. Nothing about this place seemed to resonate with Dennis' otherwise fastidious taste. The interior smelled like German Shepherds. This was a man who only traveled first class and insisted on staying in five-star hotels. He had long boasted that he had his own wing at the compound. This was true, except Denny had run out of money and Dennis' wing had been left unfinished.

Like his father, Denny also had traveled the world. He had grown up in Mexico and spent time in France. He dabbled in careers as a musician, nightclub manager and model. Denny also straightened his hair. When I first met him I thought it might be his natural texture, but I quickly learned that was not the case. I had not encountered many black men of my age who straightened their hair, and it struck me as a little peculiar.

Denny was only a year younger than me. He talked to me a bit about his father and it seemed that their relationship had never been simple. Later, he would tell me his father was a megalomaniac.

I've heard that, with fathers and sons who bear the same name there is a risk of comparison. It is said that oftentimes, the son might feel he can't live up to the name. I think this was true for Dennis and Denny. Denny had dropped out of Howard University and floundered before settling at the Guatemala compound. His father sent him a monthly 'management fee' and I think he liked being the big fish in the small pond.

Dennis' daughter, Dawn, on the other hand, was doted upon — the golden child. She had married a white doctor and became a stay-at-home mother after their children were born. Even though Dennis' relationship with Dawn was non-existent at best following her parents' divorce, Dennis loved showing off photos of his beautiful, biracial grandchildren.

I finished cleaning the bathroom and made my way back through the courtyard and into the kitchen to make myself a cup of tea. There, I stumbled upon an older African-American woman hunched over her coffee. She looked exhausted, her complexion discolored. A hard tightness around her brow made it clear that she had some work done to her face, but her neck was left untouched.

I recognized her from the day before. We had crossed paths and she had scurried off into another part of the compound without saying a word. At the time, I thought perhaps she worked there.

"Good morning," I said with a polite smile, thinking she must be the housekeeper. Maybe now we could talk about the bathroom situation.

"Hi Dori, I'm Denia Hightower," she replied as the teakettle howled to a boil.

Gotcha.

"Are you kidding me?" I thought to myself as I stared wide-eyed at Denia, caught completely off guard. I knew she would be in Guatemala for her son's wedding, but Dennis had told me she would be staying at a nearby hotel. It was suddenly crystal clear that she had intended to stay at the compound all along.

I was still uncomfortable in this new place, and now I was face-to-face with Dennis' first wife. And she had known I would be here from the start.

I was shaken, and not just from the surprise circumstances of our first meeting. I had never truly pictured Dennis as an old man. There was no denying that the woman sitting across from me at the kitchen table was an old woman. What had he done to her, I wondered?

After my surprise encounter with Denia Hightower, I could not help but feel uncomfortable, sandwiched awkwardly in the middle of Dennis' family drama, which was still a gaping wound. Knowing that I was unexpectantly sharing a house with my husband and the mother of his children to celebrate the wedding of their son felt surreal. I could sense a darker scenario.

No compound could be quite big enough for those circumstances, as far as I was concerned. This was not the friendly, modern family, post-divorce situation. This was a situation where everything did not appear to be what it seemed.

I was furious that I had been blindsided yet again. From what Dennis told me, he was completely blindsided by his son this time, too.

Then I learned that the real housekeeper was offended that I cleaned the dirty bathroom. That was it. It was time for Dennis and me to move to a hotel.

I had lain awake in the early hours of the morning, listening to the sound of the leaking bathroom faucet in Dennis' room. The rough blanket irritating my skin; I pursed my lips tightly as Dennis snored softly by my side.

Now I wondered, how could Denny have set his father up like this? Surely he knew he would be throwing his mother and his father's new wife together in an uncomfortable situation. This was just not right. We had walked straight into the lion's den.

Off to the wedding a few hours later, I slowly got dressed in the historic home where Denny's wedding was going to take place — the bride's family manor with a hotel attached. I still did not know Dennis' son well, but I knew I needed to look picture-perfect for his wedding album. That level of perfection would be my suit of armor. I decided a Brioni dress would do the trick, applied my Chanel lipstick and forced a smile in the faded bathroom mirror, only the vague outline of my face visible in its clouded surface.

The bride, Alejandra, wore black for her wedding, a tight-fitting number that featured her cleavage and matched her sleek hair. She was Guatemalan and came from a "good family."

The history and stateliness of Alejandra's ancestral home, built in the 1600's near the Santa Catalina Arch, clearly was supposed to impress the guests, but the place was crumbling around us. The electricity went out during a torrential rainstorm before the wedding.

Denia gave a toast at the reception. "Poor Denny," she gushed. "We had to move nineteen times during his childhood!"

I already knew Denny resented the moves and the fact that his father was rarely around while he was growing up. That very fact explained how the Guatemala property came to be in the first place, though eventually I found documents indicating that, by purchasing the compound for Denny to have a place to live, Dennis also was able to shelter assets during his first divorce by saying it would go to their son.

According to Dennis, Denny said, "This is mine, Mom. Don't go there. Dad and I are finally doing something together."

It seemed Dennis had gotten his son to assist in what one might assume was a scheme, all the while packaging it as father-son bonding. That man was good.

Dennis and I sat together in a place of honor near Denny and Alejandra. The pleasant sound of clinking glasses and music filled the room, expanding and swallowing up the uncomfortable space between Denia and us.

Across the crowd, I spotted her chatting with a few people, making her rounds as mother of the groom. She was headed in our direction, approaching our table, headed straight for us. She smiled and then pulled out the chair directly across from me and sat down. She smiled sweetly as I met her glance and blinked back at her, caught off guard once again. I turned to Dennis, who appeared perfectly comfortable, so I smiled, too. Dennis then rearranged the seating so I was no longer sitting directly across from his ex-wife.

I noticed the way Denia Hightower held her shoulders and styled her hair. For forty years she had hung on my husband's arm, and now she sat across from us, studying my every move. She did not look well. Life had not been kind to her.

As dinner went on, I could feel Denia's dark eyes boring into me. I was sure she was sizing up the new wife, analyzing my facial expressions and body language for any weakness or other social faux pas or signs of unhappiness. She knew the red flags; she had been married to him too, after all.

After the first course, I excused myself to find a bathroom. As I left the table, Denia called out to me.

"Dori! Dori! Don't turn on the bathroom light; it doesn't work right now!"

"Thank you for letting me know," I replied curtly.

I could only walk away from the table, poised on the outside and rattled to the core, as she smiled on. Dennis and I moved to another table for the remainder of the celebration.

The Pacaya Volcano erupted in Guatemala during our stay, and ash from the eruption shut down the airport. We had to travel with an armed guard through El Salvador to return home. By this point, I was miserable, coming undone in the brutal heat and just wanting to be back home.

A volcano seemed a fitting metaphor for our entire visit — all that anger and hurt bubbling up out of the bitter earth, pale ash pouring down over the little country like a burning rainstorm. Torrential rains and mudslides engulfed the region, and sinkholes gave away to nothingness. There was even an earthquake while we were there.

Clouds replaced the fire of Guatemala as we finally made our way back to the United States. Dennis was quiet; I could not tell if he was angry about our time in Guatemala or only disappointed that it had not lived up to his expectations. I knew that beneath his usual bravado, Dennis was frustrated and embarrassed over everything that had occurred with Denny and Denia, and I was embarrassed for him.

Regardless, I could not muster up the energy to hide my true feelings about the trip. Exactly what had he expected to happen when he played this scenario out in his head? Did he honestly believe Denny when he told him Denia would be staying at a hotel and that we would have the run of the compound? Was he as blindsided as I had been? Or did he believe I would welcome the chance to meet, or possibly one-up, his first wife? Could he not have warned me of this potential situation in advance?

Dennis and I flew home in silence. He brooded and slept most of the way, and I reflected on how good it would feel to get back to the peace and easiness that used to exist between us. We had been on edge for days, even weeks, but it would all be better back in Connecticut. I knew he still had not recovered fully from his kidney infection, but I had hoped that he finally would have a chance to rest at home.

I thought back to the few hours I had stolen early one morning in Guatemala to go to church at the Iglesia de La Merced. I walked there alone because Dennis had not wanted to go. Seeing the people coming together to worship struck me as both beautiful and curious. The affluence in Guatemala, the gold and jewels, was set out on display in the old and majestic church. Some people are so devout, they come to worship in a house of wealth and then they go home with their families, living in complete and utter poverty.

That historic church in La Antigua, with its famed Spanish Baroque architecture and magnificent columns was beautiful — devastatingly beautiful even — but one only had to look a minute longer to see the widening cracks in the façade.

A force of nature could easily bring it all down.

CHAPTER 6

THE UNRAVELING WEB

"I don't want to do this anymore; I want to be home with you, Dori," Dennis said one day.

I nodded, listening and considering what this meant for our future. I knew this revelation had been months in coming and, while I did not know exactly what had prompted his final decision, I knew he was tired. He had never quite recovered his enthusiasm for his work after his health ordeal.

"Whatever you decide," I said, "that's what we'll do."

I was in his corner, always, and trusted that this was what he needed to do next. After our difficult trip to Guatemala, maybe having more time together would be a positive thing for our marriage. We would finally have the time to settle into a routine and be together during the week. We could really travel together and go on more weekend getaways as we had planned. We would be together — a power couple. It sounded good.

Dennis resigned from his position as Deputy Secretary of Commerce in August 2010.

Eight hundred people attended the dinner where he spoke and was also honored. Oddly enough, Dennis never told me the dinner was going to be a grand event or that it was even in his honor. I just showed up at the hotel ballroom that night for business as usual. By now, I could go through the motions. I could do it all in my sleep.

I had a new makeup artist that night, and my look was much more dramatic than I was used to wearing. It was not the typical Washington, D.C. wife or the usual Connecticut conservative. I dressed flashier than usual too — a gorgeous, strapless, teal gown that shimmered under the lights and perfectly matched the color of Dennis' bowtie.

The adaptability of my look startled me. This was not my style but, by now, I could be whatever they made me — whatever the professionals decided I should be.

"Wind up and go," I repeated in my head, my traditional last-minute pep talk before heading into any function. "Just wind up and go, Dori."

I caught my reflection in the wide lobby mirror beneath the golden chandelier; I turned my head quickly left to right, checking myself from all angles. I was tired, but I did not look it.

My mask was in place.

Dennis gave a keynote address that night and I smiled demurely, shaking hands and making small talk with as many guests as I could.

I had asked him beforehand not to acknowledge me in his speech this time. He would always point me out in the room and ask me to stand. Being in the spotlight like that embarrassed me; I did not like all those eyes on me.

"Please, just do not do it this time," I asked. "Please."

He did not listen. He pointed me out anyway, and everyone craned their necks to look at Dennis' doting wife. I wanted to bolt for the door. Now I knew once and for all that his acknowledgement was not about me; it was all about him. He was just producing a sound bite to make him look like a thoughtful, humble, family man.

No one realized that he was actually a man who was making his wife feel very uncomfortable in public.

My days were all a haze by then, speeches and events running together into one frenzied blur of hair appointments and dinner speakers and baby spinach salads. Still, I wanted to pause and remember this particular dinner. This time, it was about Dennis and it was, quite possibly, the end of our journey in public service.

We would do it one more time, posing for the cameras, but the pressure was already beginning to recede, and I felt I could start to come up for air. Already, I breathed a little easier as I sipped from a chilled glass of water and posed for another set of photographs at my husband's side.

We wound down after the dinner and had a drink in the hotel lobby. As we walked away from the event that hot summer night, it was as though a weight had been lifted off my shoulders. The political life was over, and I was more than ready to turn the page to a brand new chapter — a chapter that was smaller and tidier, just Dennis, me, and our little dog, Moe. Things would be simpler now. Easy even. I was ready to say goodbye to the spotlight of Washington, D.C., and all its expectations and formalities.

I was ready to live full-time with my husband.

Dennis probably had trepidations about leaving the administration, but if he did, he never let it show on the outside; he never once wavered. I suppose it only made sense. Dennis F. Hightower had never taken a step back in his career, and he had every reason to believe he was still moving up, up, up — just changing course one more time.

In the grand tradition of the revolving door, I'm sure he figured he could just go back onto the boards of some major companies and a paid nonprofit board or two. It worked for others. People entered the administration thinking they would be golden afterwards. Dennis never conceived that it could go any other way.

He could assume a calmer lifestyle for the time being and continue to bring in a handsome sum of money. We would live comfortably in our mansion. It seemed that his options were wide open and, as always, the sky was not even the beginning of the limit for Dennis F. Hightower.

At first, having Dennis at home and being together was a dream. It was wonderful, a fresh start filled with possibilities, the kind of life I had hoped could be real when I had agreed to marry this man. After spending the first year of our marriage shuttling between cities and fitting in time for vacations, I wanted to just be home with my husband, to eat breakfast together in the morning and enjoy a simple, quiet life at Fleur D'Eau.

A few months earlier, Dennis had asked me what kind of watch I wanted for my birthday. From that point on, he talked about it all the time, showing me pictures in magazine spreads and pointing out designers he thought would suit my taste. It was classic Dennis — going shopping and making big plans.

For my birthday that summer, I opened a card from Dennis containing a "placehold-er" for a Cartier watch: a cutout picture of the watch in question taped inside. He had chosen one that I loved and it was extravagant: a $14,000 watch. I brushed the strange presentation off as usual, over-the-top Dennis, assuming he must have something planned. But what?

Dennis' return to the private sector proved rockier than I had expected. I thought that once he had some time to rest and fully recover from the past year, he could begin to bring in some money from speaking engagements. He never thought about the possibility that this could fail. Failure was simply never an option for Dennis. He was a wonderful speaker and, on the heels of his time in the administration, he had no reason to believe he would not be in high demand.

We were hopeful, but, we were mistaken. Dennis would learn quickly that the business community viewed his participation in the Obama Administration as a negative, and the speaking engagements never materialized.

"Let's protect the franchise!" I often would joke, though it was not really funny to me at all.

Dennis was our moneymaker, plain and simple. I believed in him and was committed to helping him promote his brand and make this transition to private life easier for him. I thought he had a lot to offer the world. I wanted him to write a book or go on the speaking circuit. I was working to get him on *Charlie Rose*, trying to build him up and keep his name in the public eye while we formed a strategy.

In November 2010, he asked me to borrow money from my mother to make a mortgage payment, and the following January, he was so worried about our financial situation that he mentioned maybe I could go back to work. I was too numb to process what was actually going on.

I was not against returning to my career, but I was confused. I could not help but feel resentful that he had asked me to stop working, only to ask me to start it up again just a year later. You cannot turn a legal practice on and off like a kitchen faucet. Clients would not materialize again out of thin air; the money would take time to start flowing in again, and something about the quiver in Dennis' voice told me we did not have the luxury of that sort of time.

I wondered how he had eaten through his millions so quickly. Surely, if he had been savvy enough to earn that sort of money, he must have noticed if we were living beyond our means. I still did not ask the hard questions, but I did begin pounding the pavement to get my own career back on track.

"Why don't we start a business together?" I asked him.

I thought we could provide business consulting to individuals and small businesses. We had the perfect set-up to make it happen. We could invite clients to Fleur D'Eau for retreats and help them with their business strategies. They would love it here, and we had everything in place to make it happen quickly.

I felt like his secretary some days as we plowed forward. I was making the plans and charting the course, giving it my all, while he appeared to resent having to work to build the business. I was embarrassed when he failed to follow through or make introductions. He would agree to market our business to his well-positioned contacts and then never pick up the phone.

When we had clients to Fleur D'Eau, he seemed to begrudge their presence.

For all of Dennis' success in business, I think he had the attitude that he was better than this — why should he have to chase down his money? As a result, he was not willing to put in the work to make things happen.

By May, Dennis was growing desperate and asked if he could borrow money from my mother again to pay his expenses — my mother, the retired schoolteacher, who should have been saving that money for her own future. He promised me time and again that he would pay her back, but the very idea of taking her money made me sick.

My mother wrote out another check, never to see a dollar of it repaid — $34,000 gone. Poof. Dennis turned out to be quite the magician — he could make money disappear.

I was never home.

Dennis had gone from a world where his wife was constantly waiting at home for him to return from his latest adventures, to one where he was at home and she was out trying to earn money.

This role reversal wore down his ego, and I think that being at home, rattling around in that big house, depressed him. Dennis was alone for much of the day with nothing on his agenda for the foreseeable future.

I had to work on Father's Day that year. I'm not a sentimental person when it comes to holidays, so it never crossed my mind that my absence might hurt his feelings or bruise his ego. Especially as we had no children together.

Some weeks, Dennis never left the property, staying inside for days on end.

I liked to think he was at home strategizing, working on a plan for his next great business success, something that would turn everything around and make us look back on these lean months and laugh about our worries, but that was not the case at all. He was brooding. Resentful. Captive to his own sense of impending failure and feeling the weight of his decisions bearing down on his body, which was growing older and wearier by the day.

His world was crumbling down on us.

There were moments when I thought we had turned a corner. In June, we flew to Chicago for an event at the aquarium with a consulting client. We had a nice time; that trip was the sort of lifestyle I had imagined when I thought about Dennis leaving the administration. Jetting off together, enjoying life as a power couple. Working toward the same goals. We had amazing sex the next morning.

On the flight home, Dennis began to experience an excruciating headache. His face was flushed from his neck up. I panicked, thinking he could be having a stroke. His blood pressure was through the roof by the time we arrived in Connecticut. I called his doctor. He insisted we go to the ER immediately to check things out.

As I stood in the hospital hallway waiting for updates, a nurse from the staff approached me.

"Your father will be right out," she said kindly.

"He's my husband," I replied.

"Oh, I'm sorry." Her cheeks turned red and she continued on her way.

Dennis recovered from that incident. After that I noticed he was becoming increasingly distant. He had always been a morning person, but nowadays, he would sleep in until past ten and log in long hours in his study with the door closed alone.

His body showed physical signs of his stress level. He had stopped exercising again and lost muscle tone; his teeth were looking worse by the day; and his diet was becoming strangely limited. Some days he would eat nothing but pickled herring straight from the jar.

He denied being depressed, but I could tell that he was sinking lower and lower each day. His ambition was gone. The man I married, who was always ready to take on the world, was not the man standing in front of me. This man was struggling for motivation and failing to adapt.

Nearly a full year had rolled by since Dennis had left the Obama Administration, and we had little to show for it. My husband had spent most of that time sleepwalking through his days, failing to find any sort of direction. I had spent the year worried and working and feeling largely alone. It had been a long, cold winter followed by an equally hopeless spring.

The height of summer arrived once again, and Fleur D'Eau was purring with cicadas and alive with fireflies. The Fourth of July was fast approaching and, still worried about Dennis' new career as a shut-in, I asked his cousins to invite him down to Washington, D.C., for the long weekend.

Dennis' cousin Dianne is married to a retired, four-star admiral in the United States Navy, quite possibly the only living, African-American, four-star admiral at the time. Admiral J. Paul Reason was also a Howard alumnus and a successful businessman in his own right who had sat on Walmart's board of directors.

The Reasons lived in two combined apartments in the prestigious Watergate complex, in the Foggy Bottom neighborhood of Washington — a swanky address right in the heart of the district.

I thought that getting out of the house and back to his old stomping grounds would do Dennis good, and that being around people who were still out there accomplishing things might give him the jolt he needed to rejoin the world. Finally, he agreed to go to Washington. We spent time on their boat one sunny afternoon.

Dennis was different when he returned home from that trip, but not at all in the way I had hoped.

"That's what I want," he said to me, describing their city apartment, the way they had managed to streamline their expenses and maintenance, while still enjoying the good life.

"And I always wanted a boat," he added with a disgruntled sigh.

"I didn't need this big house," I reminded him. "And I never said we couldn't have an apartment, or a boat for that matter."

I was frustrated with his attitude, especially knowing that money was tight, but I could tell that envy was overwhelming him and eating him alive — the sudden realization that he had created all of this overhead himself, a mistake he could not pass off to anyone else. The money was still pouring out through every seam, and not nearly enough was coming in.

The summer trudged on, Dennis sinking deeper and deeper into his personal abyss.

"I'm going to visit my son in Guatemala," he told me suddenly one day, one foot practically out the door.

"You're just going? Don't people who are married discuss things like that?" I asked, my hand shaking, "What's going on with you?"

Nothing.

"I guess you don't want to be married?" I added, the words spilling out of my mouth before I could even think them through.

"Actually, yes, I want a divorce."

My world stopped cold.

CHAPTER 7

THE BROKEN SPELL

A political wife. A political marriage. And in just two years, filing for a divorce.

What kind of upside-down world had I gotten myself into? Everything was in question: Why had Dennis even wanted to marry me in the first place? Why me?

He had literally begged me to marry him only months before his Senate confirmation hearing and announced he was done with our marriage about a year after leaving the administration. I could not ignore the way these two timetables had lined up perfectly, his career and our marriage.

I wonder if Dennis considered that I was a similar age to Michelle Obama. I was younger than his first wife and gave him that illusion of youth. Unlike the woman he dated before me, I was an African-American woman. Maybe with the Obamas in the White House, he felt a biracial marriage was not 'en vogue' at that particular moment.

Our first meeting in New York City might as well have been labeled an interview or audition. I now know I was not there to learn about Dennis. Dennis was there to screen me for a very specific role.

He had a list of boxes to check:

☑ Attractive   ☑ Poised

☑ Educated   ☑ African American

☑ Professional   ☑ Malleable

I met his requirements. Like Michelle Obama, I was a successful lawyer and a devoted mother. Had Dennis simply assumed the First Lady would take an interest in me? Had he envisioned us bonding over shared interests in physical fitness and the legal profession? Chatting about our daughters? Were we supposed to have become fast friends and confidantes, going to lunch in D.C. and prattling on about this week's episode of *The Good Wife* over a glass of Chardonnay? Was I simply a tool to gain access to the Obamas — another way that he could gain entry to their inner-circle?

I was at a place in my life, when we met that spring of 2009, where I was easy to mold. I was wandering without real roots, having left one life on the West Coast and not yet found a new one back East. With that freedom came an obvious vulnerability and opportunity. Dennis saw that spelled out plain on my face. My eagerness to start anew made me an easy target.

And when I had run my course, just like his time in the Obama Administration, was I, in the end, completely disposable?

☑ Disposable

We ask a lot of questions of our politicians — questions about their platform and their beliefs, presented on a stage and at a podium for all the world to see, but there is another set of questions that often goes unasked: What are you willing to give up in order to get ahead?

Whom will you destroy to make it happen? Can you look at yourself in the mirror the day after you tear them apart?

How much of your life are you ready and willing to change?

Politics does change people, but it is not always in the way we imagine. Sometimes these changes come in the back door, slight and subtle over the years; other times, they are deliberate maneuvers that we never would guess were actually politically motivated.

Dennis readily admitted that people "do better" in politics when they are married. If he intended to secure a spot in the administration and hitch his wagon to Obama's star, he believed he needed a wife. Ideally, she would be a black woman, younger than his sixty-eight years, and attractive and bright enough to impress his circle. I fit the bill, I served my purpose and now I was out.

The quarterly reviews were in and I was fired from my marriage.

I walked along our paver stone driveway, the damp morning air clinging to my bare face; a perfect disguise for the tears that refused to stop. I had hardly gotten out of bed in weeks.

I bent down to offer a dog biscuit to Moe, who had been with me every step of the way.

I paced the property. My bones felt stiff and brittle and my head ached. Was any of this real? Every day when I awoke, I half expected to find myself back in Vienna, or in the Four Seasons in Washington, fresh from my second date with a man named Dennis, simply waking from a deep and vivid dream. Back at the beginning, when everything was clean and good and new.

Instead, I was alone in a mansion and facing the swift end to my marriage.

I had not been able to eat since Dennis had left. My stomach just would not allow it. I kept picturing him in that little kitchen in Guatemala, living his life as though our entire relationship had never happened at all. Was he sipping a glass of wine while reading the paper alone at the table? Were he and his son laughing together right this very second as the volcano poised itself to erupt again?

Surely the Guatemalans were walking to Mass, the Washingtonians were waiting in the rain to catch the Metro, the Viennese stopping for coffee on their way to work. The whole world was still turning while I stood still and frozen in place.

I was broken.

It had all come on so fast. One day we were happy — so I thought — and the next, Dennis was gone. At first, I thought he was having a breakdown. I just could not fathom that he was truly finished with our marriage.

I thought he might be sick. He was close to 70 years old, he had health issues and I thought perhaps he was depressed. Could there be some diagnosis and a magical cure that would put all of this behind us?

I shivered, chilled to the bone despite the August heat.

"Come on, Muffin, let's go back inside," I called out to Moe, wiping my eyes. Moe, antagonizing the geese nearby, bounded up by my side, his fuzzy grey tail wagging in the morning sunshine. I knew he loved me, fully and completely unconditionally. He would never leave. Maybe that was all I needed to put one foot in front of the other.

I had no other choice.

August was a time of flux. I found my world turned suddenly upside-down as summer came to a close. Only this time, it was not a fairy tale of kings and castles so much as a story filled with wolves and goblins.

Dennis, seemingly unaffected by our separation, spent the month wandering ambivalently between Connecticut and Washington, D.C., and who knows where else.

He said he wanted the freedom to travel and experience the world alone, and yet he often claimed he still loved me. We still shared a bed when he was home, but argued by text message while he was away. He wanted the best of all worlds without any of the responsibilities. Chains of days spun together when nothing made sense. Feeling lost and alone, once again untethered from the world, I was all too willing to welcome him back whenever he appeared at our door.

Dennis asked me where I wanted to go for my birthday that summer. Even though we were separated, he took me to the Cloisters in New York. I love museums and had always wanted to visit this one. We held hands as we wandered among the sculptures and gardens. Things felt completely normal between us that day, our conversation was easy and our chemistry electric. It was as though the last few months had never happened.

While we were there, Dennis pulled out his Black Card and bought me a pair of emerald and pearl earrings. Why the grand gesture if he wanted a divorce?

Then he decided he wanted to become a member.

"Send the information to my place in Washington, D.C.," he said, leaning on the counter and turning away from me as he gave his information.

For the first time that day, this was not my Dennis. I did not see him simply becoming a member and all the wonderful times we would have coming back. I pictured him coming back with another woman. Maybe one he had met in Washington, D.C., who was even younger than me. Maybe they would celebrate her birthday here next year. I would be long forgotten and miles away.

"I'm a member," he would say to her as he suggested visiting the Cloisters, giving her a warm and dignified smile that would catch her and reel her in. I could see it all now, watching it happening in my head. Reality can be painful.

"I'm going out to the Vineyard for a white party," Dennis told me as he left the house one Friday.

"You're still married," I reminded him. "You think you can go out socially? Absolutely not."

He did not go.

I clung to what little was left of our relationship. I could not help it; I was still in love with the man I thought I married.

I was adamant that we would not date other people. We would respect each other through our separation and divorce. Dennis promised me the same. I thought we agreed.

"Just focus on yourself, Dori," his brother Marvin told me during those days, clearly aware of Dennis' relationship patterns. "Forget about Dennis and just move on now."

Marvin was intuitive in a way Dennis could consider to be a threat to his very existence. I think he was one of the few people who saw straight through his brother's polished exterior and evaluated the real Dennis underneath.

"Dennis has no idea of the damage he does," he said to me, always the quiet observer.

I respected Marvin and valued his honesty and insight into his brother's character. He found himself in a difficult place during Dennis' first marriage and continued to feel trapped in the middle whenever Dennis ran one of his Prince Charming games.

Only this time, I could not absorb Marvin's words. Not while I still held fast to the idea that something else had to be going on with Dennis. Devastated and searching for answers, I went with Dennis to his primary care physician in Washington, D.C., who referred us to a marriage counselor.

Part of me still wanted to attribute the breakdown of our marriage to Dennis' health. It was the only thing that made sense to me.

Soon after I returned home from our appointment with Dennis' doctor, I found a yellow Post-it note in the top of a wastebasket in Dennis' study. On it, he had scrawled three words: "renal cell carcinoma." Cancer. My throat tightened.

"Of course," I thought. "That's what this is all about."

Since his nerve-sparing radial prostatectomy, Dennis went in for regular blood tests to check the status of his prostate-specific antigen (PSA), a protein that is elevated in men with prostate cancer. I soon learned that his numbers were slowly climbing and he faced the very real possibility of radiation if his continued to rise.

Prostate cancer is often a slow process, and Dennis had a lot of time to think about the possibility that his cancer would be back, and anticipate the oncoming battle. This must be it. The prospect of facing prostate cancer for a second time explained his erratic behavior to my broken heart.

I knew now that Dennis was scared. Clearly he was searching for answers, thinking he was much sicker than he ever let on. Still, I felt as though I was not seeing the complete picture and was left with more questions than answers.

During marriage counseling, I began to get my answers about Dennis' health and other questions I had held onto quietly, questions that had plagued me since our long week at George Washington University Hospital when he had the septic infection.

I also learned Dennis had been diagnosed with a brain aneurism. This very fact made him nearly uninsurable. The idea of being uninsurable was news to me at the time. I was in my 40s; you don't think about the possibility of being uninsurable when you are young and healthy. You know insurance is more expensive if you are in poor health, but you do not give it much additional thought. You do not think about the consequences of ill health — at least, I know I did not.

He had kidney stone episodes and had been suffering from renal insufficiency for a long time. He had blood in his urine and chronic diarrhea. I had no idea kidney stones would affect his health for the rest of his life. He never told me.

His flushed face and constant back pain were side effects of Cialis.

"What Cialis?" I had no idea at the time he was using erectile dysfunction medication.

He had hidden his reliance on Cialis from me throughout our marriage. "Let me know if I ever need it," he once said with a teasing wink.

He had playfully instructed me to be honest with him; I had not bargained on the fact that honesty was not one of his virtues.

He made light of it, but all the while he was popping his little yellow pills like after-dinner mints in the next room.

When you're marrying a man who is significantly older and already has underlying health issues, you expect he may have trouble in bed. I knew it was a fact of life, and Dennis could have just been honest with me from the start — it would have been okay. Instead he was hiding his health conditions and medication, completely disregarding the health risks that came with using Cialis.

He had experienced side effects from Cialis for our entire marriage: paralyzing pain, headaches, body pains, upset stomach and nausea. Once, while we were staying at the St. Regis Hotel in New York City, we'd had sex that left him so sick, he could not attend his board meeting for Accenture. I had not understood what had happened then, but once I knew that he was taking Cialis, it made sense. Dennis was making himself sick with the pills, but he continued using them to save his pride in the bedroom.

"Why didn't you just tell me?" I said to him quietly, my eyes fixed on the carpet, mentally tracing the pattern.

The full account of his health was finally out on the table.

I knew that his erectile dysfunction had been a hot topic in his first marriage, or so he said, and he claimed his first wife had berated him about sex. I wanted to remain calm; I did not want to push him, but I could not stand knowing he had been so reckless, so irresponsible and, worse still, that he had faced it alone and kept this secret from me.

"I did not think you would marry me if you knew," Dennis replied simply.

The reality was that I would not have cared. I loved him and would have married him even if I had known. But I was realizing that he had not felt the same about me.

Why did he want to get married so quickly? Once bits of truth started slipping out, it seemed like there was no stopping it. My entire relationship with Dennis was bursting open at the seams, all the lies pouring out into the open, our whole life together disintegrating into fragments, into nothingness.

"Our marriage counselor asked me what was going on before I married you," Dennis said to me one day after a separate session. His words were acidic, stinging with every syllable, just as he intended them to be. "So I just wanted you to know I married you on the rebound."

He and his former girlfriend broke up not long before the Accenture board meeting in New York City, the day before we met at the London Hotel. He had never let on that the break-up was so recent, or that he had long-term relationships following his first marriage. I assumed he had girlfriends, of course, but nothing serious.

Dennis was forthcoming with other shocking surprises, too, thanks to the counselor. Next he came clean about Fleur D'Eau.

His financial situation was not what he claimed, he said. The truth was complicated, he said.

I had never truly owned our home, but neither, it turned out, had Dennis. He had borrowed every penny to pay for it through banks and, when it sold, everything would go towards settling his debts.

I was shattered. I felt as though anything and everything he had told me could suddenly turn out to be a lie. First the reason he married me, then the ownership of Fleur D'Eau…what would be next? Everything was in question.

I lay awake nights replaying Dennis' revelations in my head — his health problems, Cialis, his finances, our home, "I married you on the rebound" — until they blurred together into one enormous two-year lie. I had changed my life for him, changed myself for him, and I was finding out that nothing was ever real at all.

The Dennis I knew, the Dennis I thought I married, had not really existed at all.

Had Dennis believed his own stories and used his imagined power to rake in more friends, more money, more résumé fodder? Did these stories catapult him straight into the upper echelons of power?

OMG - He had done it right before my eyes.

I was relaxing and trying to sleep in our bedroom one night in early October when my phone rang.

I saw Dennis' name on the screen and answered his call. That morning he had seen our marriage counselor in D.C. and we had a reasonably pleasant day. Despite some of the things that had been said, we were still civil to each other.

This time, however, Dennis had not called me to go over interest penalties or discuss mortgage payments. In fact, he had not meant to call me at all, although our marriage was indeed the topic of conversation when I answered the phone.

"Could you believe it?" I heard him say. "What kind of wife she was — she wouldn't move to Washington, D.C. to be with her husband when I was in the Obama Administration. What kind of wife was she?"

Here he was referring to me as his ex-wife when in fact neither of us had even filed for divorce yet!

He had butt-dialed me while on a date with a woman he had met on a well-known hook-up website. He was now casually appraising me to this other woman over wine and hors d'oeuvres.

I continued to listen. I heard her offer him wine and peach cobbler.

"You and me, 'Peaches Cobbler', we have more years behind us on the runway than we have ahead of us," he said seductively.

"Who is Peaches Cobbler?" I thought, sitting bolt upright.

Whoever she was, Peaches Cobbler was buying every word of his self-pity and heartbreak, exuding sympathy for this poor, wronged man. She invited him upstairs to her bedroom after aperitifs and I continued to listen in. I heard them chuckling, kissing and discussing their plans to go away for the weekend before Dennis' phone finally beeped out of power.

I sat frozen in the darkness of the palatial bedroom Dennis and I had shared, on the enormous, king-sized sleigh bed he had bought for us, an exact replica of the bed he had in Washington, D.C. Everything from the silk duvet to the gold pillows dripped with opulence, but right then it all felt worthless.

My heart raced. Even though we had been separated for months, the finale had never been so crystal clear. This moment marked the end.

Not only was it over. It really had all been a lie.

I had just listened quietly for an hour-and-a-half as Dennis demeaned me while he cheated on me. I heard him seduce Peaches Cobbler with the very same lines he had once used on me. Word for word, he reused his lines without any ounce of care or sincerity.

"I am so comfortable with you," I heard him say. "We don't have to have sex right now — I just want to hold you."

He told her they would go away to a lodge in Shenandoah, the very same romantic weekend he had once planned for me. He was playing her, just as he had done with me. I recognized every word, every syllable of his old routine. He was not very original.

I turned on the bedside lamp, illuminating the rich, golden hue of our bedroom, a place I had once felt was fit for a king and queen. Now I saw that, while Dennis was skilled at making me feel like a queen, he was hardly a king.

I felt myself shaking. Was it panic? Was it rage? Was it simply disgust? Had my entire marriage to this man been built on empty words and utter lies?

My head ached with the weight of my new reality.

Sleep would not be an option that night. I was focused. I tried calling Marvin, but he did not answer his phone. He had warned me the last time we spoke that Dennis could not be alone, and I think he knew that night that Dennis had gone out on a date. It was the last time I tried to contact Marvin.

Next, I called my parents and told them what had just happened.

"Don't let him know you know," they told me.

I knew what they were saying, but I could not do it. I was too angry to be strategic.

Dennis called me again, just after two in the morning. This time intentionally. I figured his brother told him I was blowing up his phone and warned him that he better call me. Overtired and devastated, my head still reeling from everything I heard earlier, I confronted him.

"Who is Peaches Cobbler?" I asked.

"I don't know any Peaches Cobbler." he replied quickly.

"Do not insult my intelligence with your lies; I do not deserve this," I said. "How dare you!"

He was silent, reflecting, I suppose, on being found out.

"So what are you going to do about it?" he said, his voice mixed with derision and calm, as if I was not his wife…as if I were nothing at all.

I pictured his face on the other end of the line. The warm brown eyes creased with familiar little lines, the nose I had admired in profile, and the lips I had kissed on our wedding day and so many times since. Yet, somehow, the man I pictured, the man whose voice echoed into the phone, was hollow. This Dennis was a stranger to me, just an empty mask.

"I will think about it," I said, as calmly as I could manage, and I hung up the phone.

My family rallied around me as I fell apart. My father had always been skeptical of Dennis, but he had put his concerns aside for my happiness. It was my mother, a kind woman we jokingly call 'Saint Jean', who was the first to have had enough.

"This is eating you up, Dori," she said to me one day as we sat around the kitchen table discussing my next steps. "Are you going to let this fucking man destroy you? He is not worth it."

I wanted to believe in Dennis, believe in the dream life he had sold me and the man he had pretended to be — the man who had loved me passionately and deeply. Maybe I chose to stifle my doubts and intuitions because part of me did not want that fantasy to end. It was not because of the money or the lifestyle; it was the idea of a man like Dennis sweeping me off my feet. The fantasy of a once-in-a-lifetime romance.

My mother was right — this fucking man was not worth the anguish.

Her words were just the jolt I needed to break the spell. As the raw, debilitating pain of loss began to recede and the numbness of my mind ebbed, in came curiosity. Not just any kind of curiosity, but a compelling need to understand what exactly had happened to me. I needed to figure out what had happened to bring our relationship to such a swift and bitter end.

I remembered a phone call I received one day early that summer almost two years after we married. It was one of Dennis' ex-girlfriends, whom I just happened to know before I met him.

"Hi Dori, just calling to see how you're doing," she said, her voice shrilly charming. "Congratulations on getting married!"

I knew Amaretta Stone. We live in a small world and I had met her at a conference for the Black Entertainment and Sports Lawyers Association. A once successful musician, she met Dennis when they were children at Camp Atwater in Massachusetts, a prominent summer camp for children of African-American professionals. Dennis taught her to swim that summer, and she said at one point that she had always been in love with him. It is no wonder he kept her around — her wide-eyed schoolgirl worship played squarely into his inflated ego.

As far as I was concerned, they were simply too old to still be playing games.

And now Amaretta Stone and I were exchanging pleasantries on the phone like we were old friends. Like we had shared a bunk at summer camp. The conversation felt strange and programmed. Even at the time, I felt like something was wrong with the situation. Why did she think to call me out of the blue like that? Were she and Dennis still in touch?

Looking back, I wonder if Dennis had asked her to call me up just to screw with my mind. It would not have been the first time he used Amaretta Stone to pull a stunt like that.

Amaretta Stone had testified in Dennis' first divorce, when she was identified as his paramour. His first wife had her deposed because she found evidence that Amaretta Stone had been in their Parisian apartment: clothing left behind, a carefully placed tube of lipstick in a cabinet and shower scrub in the bathroom. It was a trail of possessions so obvious that one reasonably might think Amaretta Stone and Dennis wanted them to be found out.

"I confronted Dennis about it later that day. "Why is Amaretta Stone calling me?" I pressed. "If she calls here again, I am going to let her have it."

"Dori, let it go," he responded, a touch too calmly. "Just don't give her the satisfaction."

He was the very picture of self-righteous innocence — maybe a bit too innocent for it to be real. Dennis had many wonderful qualities in my eyes, but naïve innocence was not one of them.

Businessmen and politicians like Dennis must be contrivers and planners, able to strategize and think ten steps ahead of their opponents to succeed. These men do not just turn those traits off at home. They cannot. They either already possessed these qualities at the beginning of their careers or they learned them so well that manipulation became ingrained in their identity.

Amaretta Stone already had sabotaged one marriage, rattled his poor ex-wife, and forced her to look at his actions and their future square in the eye. I did not put it past him to use her again.

What was I going to do about it?

CHAPTER 8

THE NOSE THAT GROWS

Dennis once told me that, when he was a child, he would sometimes walk down to the neighborhood candy store with his friends. He went there with one goal in mind: stealing comic books.

Finally, someone caught him in the act and he had to answer for his actions. His take-away from this experience was not anything about honesty or morality. No, Dennis had learned that he would have to get better at not being caught and, if he ever did get caught, he would have to find a way out.

Now, Dennis was scrambling. He totally underestimated me. When attacked, it is my nature to fight back in order to protect myself. How had Dennis never realized that? After all the hours he had spent questioning Lisa about me, studying me, preparing to make his move, after all the days we had spent together during the past two years, how could he have expected me to be the meek little Stepford Wife going to yoga classes and waiting around, ready at his beck and call passively up in Connecticut? That was not me at all.

Had he mistaken me for a woman who would simply accept being manipulated, used, destroyed and discarded? Had he somehow gotten off on that added risk? Could the idea of pulling one over on a divorce attorney have somehow energized and intrigued him — a challenge he could not resist? Did he honestly think he could get away with the lies and manipulations? I would like to think that there are consequences for the actions of a man like Dennis F. Hightower, but to date they have yet to be enforced.

I may have been blinded temporarily, but I knew what lies and betrayals looked like. They are the common threads that run throughout divorce cases. I knew the warning signs from working with clients; not only do I practice family law, I had already become acquainted with the warning signs personally when my first marriage succumbed to lies.

I believed I would be wiser the second time I married, but I was caught up in the glow of a fairy tale. Surely Prince Charming would not act like a scoundrel. Not in this marriage; not with this man.

Yet somehow, I was the only one surprised by the outcome.

I told Dennis' cousin Dianne that he wanted a divorce.

"Oh, not this again," she replied without hesitation.

I did not hear from her after Dennis and I separated, short of an email to wish me good luck, closing out that chapter. They were Dennis' family, after all, and no matter what happened between us, they would have to align themselves with him after our marriage ended. It is just the way these things play out.

According to Dennis, Dianne and the Admiral lent him the $15,000 he needed for his attorney's retainer.

Before the day Dennis left for Guatemala, I had believed everything he ever told me about himself and about our marriage. I believed it at face value. I never checked his phone. I never snooped through his things or eavesdropped on a phone call. I never thought I had any reason to snoop.

Now, with his 11 p.m. butt dial fresh in my mind, all bets were off.

Difficult situation – "Think with your head not your heart." I repeated this over and over to myself.

Driven by a tremendous need to understand what had happened to my marriage, I began the slow process of going through all the files and documents Dennis left behind in the house — a careful excavation into the dark underworld of our life together.

"Think with your head, not your heart," I told myself. I knew what I had to do.

I began in his dark, mahogany-laden study, opening the blinds to let the sunlight pour back into the place where he had spent so much of his time in Connecticut. I could still picture him in the room, surrounded by his corporate memorabilia and plaques: a shrine to Dennis F. Hightower.

The Dennis I knew had demanded military-level neatness, with everything exactly in its place at all times, and yet his study told a completely different story. I noticed he had never fully unpacked. Not only that, his files were scattered everywhere, wads of documents and files stuffed into old brown paper bags.

They defied any filing system, papers turning up in unlikely places, everything mixed in together. I sat, tucking my legs beneath me on the floor, and began sifting through envelopes and reading over bills. Piles of paperwork spread out across tables and floors, and I had to fight the urge to trash it all. They churned and spun, creating thick whirlpools until I felt seasick.

"Who are you, Dennis F. Hightower?" I whispered under my breath to no one at all. I was alone listening to the complete and aching silence of a big house — ten thousand square feet of empty dreams.

Dennis told me at the end of our relationship that he always enjoyed having secrets and knowing things other people did not know. Now, I was poised to uncover those secrets.

Apparently, Dennis did not throw anything away. I found letters his first wife had written to her friends and her attorney, explaining the circumstances surrounding their separation. How did he get his hands on them?

I held my breath as I continued to search through Dennis' desk.

As the discovery process went on in the divorce, I was approved to take Denia's deposition. My goal would have been to find further discrepancies and places where his financial representations did not add up. Then, in October 2013, Dennis filed for bankruptcy in Washington, D.C. Our divorce was suspended and a bankruptcy stay was put into effect. Denia's deposition would be delayed for three years.

When I finally deposed Denia Stukes Hightower on July 5, 2016, in a conference room near Dupont Circle in Washington, D.C., neither Dennis nor his attorney attended. Dennis was in the hospital for an undisclosed illness, according to his lawyer.

The information we gleaned from the deposition regarding the assets and the house in Guatemala would be admissible at trial. However, I had to incur close to $18,000 in legal fees because both Dennis' and Denia's attorneys had vigorously sought to block her from being deposed.

Denia's attorneys objected to the deposition on the grounds that she was "elderly, frail, suffering from neurological deficits, had been emotionally damaged by her divorce, and had difficulty with time and spatial relationships." It was an invalid legal argument — the legal standard allowed for the deposition *as long as the information sought could lead to admissible information.*

When Denia arrived at the deposition almost a half-hour late she was with her daughter Dawn, who assisted her in walking and guided her into the conference room. At age seventy-five, the woman at Denny's wedding now appeared significantly older. She wore multiple rings on three fingers of each hand; she twisted the rings and slid them on and off her skeletal fingers. She wore a large, diamond solitaire ring that needed a cleaning. Her engagement ring from Dennis perhaps?

I noticed other details as I waited for the deposition to begin: the heels of her shoes were worn down, her grey roots were visible and one of her stockings was ripped.

Flanked by her attorney and Dawn, Denia under oath denied having been diagnosed with any mental deficits or taking any medications.

The deposition began. Denia frequently lamented being there and appeared truly bewildered about why she was being questioned over a chapter of her life she had put behind her years before. She testified that she did not recall when she was married, how long she was married or the year she was divorced.

During the deposition, Denia did not recognize her own handwriting, the handwriting of her former husband of 42 years, the divorce decree she signed and just about any document put before her, all of which she refused to read.

Much to my surprise, I really did not know what to expect, but discrepancies and inconsistencies between Dennis' sworn testimony in our divorce proceedings and Denia's statements soon became apparent.

Specifically, Dennis had testified that he made a lump sum alimony payment of $70,000 to Denia in 2014, resulting from an agreement he made with her attorney to defer alimony payments. However, Denia testified that did not happen — if Dennis had not made the monthly payments, she would have said something about it. Despite the fact that she had received monthly alimony payments for five years, she failed to remember if she received a check or if the payments were wired into her account.

Dennis also testified during his deposition that Denny had moved out of the Guatemala house in 2013 and that he had lived in two other places since then. Denia, on the other hand, testified that Denny was still living in the same house he had lived in since he married in May 2010 and that she had visited him there, but that he was now renting it from the new owner.

Denia also said she was not aware that Dennis owned any property in Guatemala when she was still married to him in 2006. Her attorney reviewed the documents we offered, which noted Dennis' ownership of the Guatemala property. Dennis had signed those papers under oath and penalty of perjury or other criminal sanctions, causing Denia's lawyer to remark, "Maybe we need to go after him," since he had failed to disclose his ownership of the Guatemala property at the time of her divorce.

I left the deposition deeply disturbed, my soul heavy. I had not intended to hurt Denia or her daughter. As a daughter myself, I understood Dawn's desire to protect her elderly mother from more mental anguish. As the estranged wife of Dennis F. Hightower, I also understood the pain his actions caused Denia, and I empathized with her.

As the one fighting for my due in my own proceedings, I was frustrated and exhausted from the obstreperous shenanigans of Denia, Dennis and Denny, either intentional or unintentional. I wanted to know the truth. I left the deposition not knowing who was lying. But someone was clearly not telling the truth.

There were lies on top of lies on top of more endless lies. Some were intentional, others motivated by self-protection and resentment against me. It was clear Dennis' lies were beginning to unravel, and one would think that would make me feel better. That I would get a sense of personal satisfaction for being "right." But that was not the case.

During her deposition, one of Denia's letters, which she denied ever writing even though it was in her handwriting, was called into question. Whether she had blocked it out or just did not recall I can only leave open to speculation. In the letter someone wrote *"But none of you who care about Dennis could ever imagine what it is like to see someone who was decent, caring, moral and honorable become someone so different."*

My heart sank. I could imagine it only too well.

In the letter's margins, in his familiar, block-letter handwriting, Dennis had provided a running commentary, underlining sections and tearing apart her words, adding insults and making excuses for his utterly inexcusable actions and behavior.

He corrected years and dates, recalculating her math. He labeled entire sections "B.S." or "Victim Syndrome," and "Her view, not shared by all as she wants to believe."

The Dennis on these pages was not the loving and charismatic gentleman I had married. He was not chivalrous or remotely kind. Instead, I was reading the mean spirited comments of an angry, entitled, bitter little man.

In Denia's letter, she wrote that Dennis had called her friends to tell them his side of their divorce. Who does something like that and for what purpose? Hurling petty insults at the woman with whom he had spent more than forty years and raised two children?

The Bracelet

Dennis gave me a beautiful antique diamond bracelet as a wedding gift.

In May 2011, after Dennis told me we were having financial problems, I noticed the bracelet was missing. It was around the time we took a trip to Atlanta, Georgia, for a Black Enterprise event where Dennis was a speaker. I was sad — it was a beautiful piece and had significant sentimental value because it was his wedding present to me.

We reported the loss to the insurance company, and Dennis received a check for $25,000, which he deposited in his account. Much to my surprise, on one of my post-separation explorations in Fleur D'Eau, I found the bracelet in the cedar closet on the lower level of the house, inside Dennis' golf bag.

Anxious and out of breath, my heart pounding, I called my lawyer and told him I found the bracelet that Dennis had reported as missing to our insurance company. I was worried that Dennis was trying to set me up for insurance fraud — what other credible explanation could there be for a $25,000 diamond bracelet to be tucked into a golf bag in a storage closet?

I offered to turn the bracelet over to the insurance company, but according to my lawyer, they declined. My attorney then followed up again with both Dennis and the insurance company, but neither responded. I did not hear another word about the bracelet... until recently.

While reviewing Dennis' bankruptcy submissions, I saw that he reported a settlement with the insurance company and paid them back for the money he received for the recovered property. I had no way to verify if this was true or not. I truly did not know what to believe.

On another hunt, I found a memory card from a digital camera, tucked behind Dennis' unused checks. I went to a local FedEx/Kinko's store and printed out the photos, which showed Dennis and his ex-girlfriend, the one that he claimed had sent him on a rebound to me. Lo and behold, my $25,000 diamond bracelet, his wedding gift to me, sparkled on her wrist. A familiar pearl and diamond necklace that he had also given to me hung around her neck.

She never looked happy in the photographs, but there she was. What's more, she was posing the same way and in the same locations where Dennis had so carefully arranged me for the camera. She was leaning in to smell a bouquet of Esperanza roses, my favorites, and hanging onto his arm in the very same restaurant where we had spent a romantic evening.

Staring at the photos, I felt as though the whole time Dennis and I had been together, he had been reliving a fantasy, her story and his time with her, repeating the same patterns. He had not started a new chapter when we met — he continued his old one, simply swapping out the leading lady.

Those were also my thoughts that day at the Cloisters when I distinctly felt Dennis was priming for the next victim to woo and replace in his photos and favorite haunts.

He took me to all the same restaurants, requesting the very same tables, ordering the same bottles of wine. He posed me in the same manner in hotel lobbies, crossing her name neatly out and writing my name in her place as if she had meant nothing at all.

Even my engagement ring, with its three stones, bore an undeniable resemblance to his ex-girlfriend's three-stone ring.

I wondered for a brief and awful moment if Amaretta Stone would be the next one to take our place next. No, Dennis kept her around for his ego, but then I remembered him also telling me that their relationship never went further because she had a bad reputation.

My search in the house we had once shared continued, revealing layer upon layer of lies and doubts and even more questions. Quite honestly I continued to search for clues to gain insight into what had happened in my marriage until the day I was forced to leave.

As I unfolded another piece of paper, I saw that it was a divorce decree. I read the names printed across the top: Dennis Fowler Hightower and Dori Bye Hightower.

"How is that possible?" I thought. How could he forge a divorce decree? Who is this psychopath? The more I read about psychopaths, it had seemed to me Dennis followed that pattern, and I was his latest victim.

I could barely breathe. Once again, I ran to the phone to call my lawyer as my heart was palpitating outside of my chest.

My jaw dropped as I realized the decree was dated July 7, 2010. That was the month before he had left the Obama Administration and less than a year into our marriage.

Looking a little closer, I could see the document was a forgery, and not even a very good one at that — it looked to be a Connecticut document, but it was in a format used in Washington, D.C. Upon closer examination, I saw it was almost an exact replica of another divorce decree, bearing the signature of Judge Michael Ryan, the very same Washington, D.C. judge who had signed Dennis' and Denia's divorce decree. Dennis had used the document from his first divorce as a template. He substituted my name and a new date, kept the D.C. format and created a fabrication. The decree even included a forged signature of a deputy clerk of the Connecticut Superior Court.

I struggled to understand the motive behind this forgery. Did Dennis already want a divorce that summer, so soon after we were married? I imagined him checking out how our names looked on the page, trying a second divorce on for size like a new tuxedo.

Or was it more sinister than that. Why had he needed this? Then I thought of another reason for a forged decree? I wondered who in his life had perhaps needed proof that I was about to be out of the picture? If he had used the forgery, he must have been trying to convince someone that our marriage was over and that I had no claim against our property.

I could only surmise.

Once I began digging, there was no coming back. I had fallen down the rabbit hole and found myself in a world where nothing was as it appeared.

My name is on the title for Fleur D'Eau, but in October 2011, Dennis told me I was not entitled to a single cent because it really belonged to his buddies who loaned him the money for it.

We had been to his compound in Guatemala, but he denied having an interest in any home there.

The annual financial disclosure the FBI used to vet Dennis for his role in the Department of Commerce contained glaring statements that were inconsistent with his representations in the divorce and bankruptcy cases. He testified at a hearing before the United States Bankruptcy Court District of Columbia on December 2, 2015, before the Honorable S. Martin Teel, Jr.:

Attorney Lynn: Do you recall a time when you were nominated by the President to be the U.S. Deputy Secretary of Commerce?

Dennis F. Hightower: Yes, I do. Yes, indeed.

Attorney Lynn: Do you recall showing on that form, that you had an ownership interest in a property in Guatemala?

Dennis F. Hightower: Yes.

Attorney Lynn: Why did you do that?

Dennis F. Hightower: Basically, it was advice, which now, clearly, it was bad advice, that I was given —

Basically, it was advice that I was given by a group of people in the White House who typically shepherd these kinds of nominations.

(Hearing Transcript December 2, 2015 at page 51 lines 2 – 19)

We supposedly had a lot of money, a lot of luxurious things, but I did not really have anything at all.

In a world built entirely on illusion, what was real?

I continued to work slowly for a few hours each day until I needed to step away and clear my head. Over the next several years, a web of lies and deceit spread out around me, a vast web of facts and fraud and names — a tangle that was as richly complex as it was absolutely deceitful.

I learned that Dennis never filed his annual financial disclosure in 2010 as Deputy Secretary of Commerce. I tried to get access to it through the Freedom of Information Act and was informed that he never filed it. I thought the disclosure was a requirement for someone with his position in the government. How had he once again gotten away unscathed? I didn't know what to believe.

In October 2013, with just a few months to go before our divorce was scheduled for trial in Connecticut, Dennis filed for bankruptcy in Washington, D.C. About a year and a half later, appraisers sent by the Bankruptcy Trustee arrived, and I could do nothing but lean against my kitchen doorway and watch as they walked through the rooms of Fleur D'Eau, sifting through Dennis' prized collections — the bronze and silver, and of course his beloved jade — to evaluate its worth.

The appraiser squinted, furrowing his brow in a way that told me he did not like what he was seeing, not one bit. The so-called legacy items claimed as sterling silver was merely silver-plated and the cherished crystal could be purchased at any Home Goods.

"These original appraisal documents, the ones from 1995, are clearly forgeries," he said. "Look at how the three in this $30,000 overlaps with the first zero."

I nodded. I saw it too, of course, and I had a bad feeling about where this was headed.

"Now see how there is a blotch under it? And how all the numbers, here…" the appraiser flipped back through the notepad, his thin mouth frowning as he found his place again. "And the $50,000 line is all wavy and the five here is smudged."

"How many of the documents do you think have been altered this way?" I asked, glancing around the room at Dennis' little museum. I was afraid I already knew the answer to my question. I already had learned that most of our lifestyle was one grand illusion. A sleight of hand. An entire life of possessions built on smudged ink and misrepresentations.

Weeks later the complete assessment of Dennis' priceless collection arrived in my mailbox in a plain white envelope. As I had expected, the numbers were not anywhere close to what Dennis had claimed.

- A jade tray: estimated value $700.00, offer $350.00.

- A jade horse: estimated value $5,000.00, offer $2,000.00.

- A jade screen: estimated value $2,000.00, offer $1,000.00.

The list went on and on, citing values that were less than half of what Dennis had reported to the insurance company.

As baffling as it was to learn the appraiser's findings about the appraisals Dennis furnished to him, on top of all the other remnants of forgery, it was still difficult to comprehend and digest. What was his motivation? Had he planned on destroying his treasured collections someday in order to collect on the higher insured value? That did not seem consistent with the way he babied his possessions, particularly his collection of jade, displaying them and fawning over them and showing them off in great detail to anyone who would listen. But then again, who knows?

Was it possible that the truth was stranger still? Had he needed to go the distance to pretend his treasures were as priceless as he wanted them to be, as valuable as they were in his own imagination? Propping up his ego with paperwork, he would have something tangible to back up his stories. Words on a page were worth more than cheap jade. He had forged the documents, and now he had yet another piece of paper to file away. A piece of paper that would tell him he was special.

The mounting evidence of deception was sickening. Dennis F. Hightower had sat on Air Force Two with Vice President Joe Biden. He was FBI-vetted, a titan of business. He presented himself as a pillar of dignity and integrity, yet he was anything but. He hid behind his credentials as if they protected him from all consequences.

As a Presidential appointee, he had already deceived the FBI, the President of the United States and the U.S. government through false statements on his background documentation for the position of Deputy Secretary of Commerce, and now he had deceived me. There was no more room for denial. No going back.

As I wandered the halls of Fleur D'Eau late that night, the deafening stillness closing in, I thought about Dennis' African art — his collection of intricate masks that stared down at me from the walls. They could have been cheap replicas, for all I knew. It would have been laughable, if it had not been so destructive.

These macabre painted pieces with their dark colors and ritualistic, vibrant patterns were once a part of Dennis' story of his life — his tale of gallivanting about the globe. I had listened adoringly, of course, and played right into his trap, eating up every word of his glory days.

Precisely as he had wanted.

Now the masks seemed to haunt me from their sturdy mounts, staring down at me with an ominous mocking arrangement, as if to say: "He's been wearing a mask this entire time."

So much of Dennis' identity was wrapped up in his perceived wealth. He presented himself as a man of substance and sophistication. From the way he dressed to the way he ordered his meals in restaurants, he kept up the façade of class.

Dennis had not grown up wealthy. His family was decidedly middle-class — his father worked for the post office, his mother was a teacher — but Dennis had quickly pulled himself up through the business ranks so that, by the time I met him, he was accustomed to an affluent lifestyle.

Against my mother's advice, I had closed my practice during our marriage and become entirely reliant on Dennis financially. I had transformed myself into the kind of wife he wanted, the kind who would be best suited to support his career, but it was not sustainable. Unbeknownst to me at the time, we were living off of loans and his hot air.

The layers of deceit were thick — I could not tell where his entire charade began.

With the end of our marriage came the end of illusions. On paper, Dennis was flat broke. He was in worse shape than I had been when we first met, and he had been for some time.

At one point during the year we spent struggling for money, Dennis told me he was thinking of selling the house in Washington to pay our bills. He asked me to help him find a way to evict Marvin in order to sell the home.

I learned that would not have helped us anyway. The truth was Dennis already had taken out a home equity loan on the house and racked up so much debt that he would not gain anything at all from selling the Washington home. By pretending to take action, he was just further covering his tracks, pretending he did not have the debt and that it was an asset.

Furthermore, he did not even own the entire house. He had a half-interest, and his brother owned the other half. Seriously, the man played me about throwing his own brother out of the house that they owned jointly. Even on his financial disclosures, which he signed under penalty of perjury, he claimed he owned 100 percent of the D.C. property.

Was Dennis loyal to anyone other than himself?

I began to wonder just how long ago he had been worth millions. He had not been honest about how much he had retained in his first divorce — claiming it was $8 million when it was actually $1 million — and he had conveniently omitted his history of taking out loans from friends.

So why would anyone ever have pledged their personal collateral for close to $2 million for our home? In reality, Dennis may not have had the financial ability to qualify for a $3,562,000 home.

He told me at the time that he had taken money for the down payment for our house out of a fund invested by Eddie C. Brown, an old friend from his days at Howard

University. Brown was the founder of Brown Capital Management in Baltimore. It is one of the largest minority-owned investment firms in the United States and Dennis was a member of the Board of Trustees.

As I searched through the mass of papers Dennis left behind, I discovered the source of Dennis' down payment on our home based on written loan documentation. According to those documents, the down payment loan was made possible by his buddy Eddie putting up the collateral using his own T. Rowe Price stock to the tune of approximately $1.6 million on Dennis' behalf, and then Harbor Bank of Maryland with James Haskins, a business associate of Eddie's at the helm, made the loan a reality. The down payment deal was finalized for a commercial property, which our house was not. But then again who knows? At the time, Eddie Brown and James Haskins were among the prominent minority-business owners in Baltimore that had been tapped to participate in the redevelopment of the $1.5 billion State Center office complex.

Why would a man like Eddie Brown do that for Dennis? The signed documents were staring me in the face but none of it made any sense.

It appeared from so many of the details that it all looked suspect. For a time, he had the mortgage coupons sent to his Washington address so he would never have to worry that I would open something and learn a little too much. In the Connecticut closing document for the house, Dennis failed to disclose the existence of the Harbor Bank of Maryland loan as the source of the down payment for our Connecticut home. Was that not a violation of the 2009 HUD-1 form requirements? Mortgage fraud is sometimes defined as the intentional omission of the true source of funds for the down payment. In addition, the Harbor Bank loan was classified as a commercial loan when it was not. It is still hard to believe and yet this did appear to be an example of loan application fraud.

It all made me further wonder what kind of monster I had married.

I also learned that Dennis was receiving a questionable income stipend from Eddie. After he left the administration, Eddie paid him $6,666.67 a month as an incentive for Dennis to introduce Brown Capital Management to his contacts. The monthly payments were wired directly into our joint Citibank account.

In September 2011, Eddie loaned Dennis another $200,000. Dennis also told me Eddie had been making many of the Harbor Bank of Maryland loan payments on his behalf.

Some of the other 'loans' Dennis received while he was part of the Obama Administration were from other prominent players in the business world.

It was not enough for me to just know where the money was coming from; I needed to know the full extent of the situation. Was any of this legal? During the divorce discovery process several of Dennis' 'friends' were deposed.

Eddie refused to answer my questions about his personal relationship with Dennis and the money he was giving him. He also refused to produce all the documents requested but made the mistake of bringing some of them with him to his deposition. Anything you bring into the deposition is fair game and my attorney was able to ask for copies of the documents he had not wanted to produce.

Some of the documents obtained contained fraudulent representations of the Fleur D'Eau's purchase. They confirmed that the loan was miscategorized as money for a "commercial investment property." Even our address was misrepresented, listing only two out of the three digits of the street address.

Later, Eddie sued Dennis. I don't think I will ever know if he did this only to save face once I began asking questions, after it was noted that he had done nothing to collect the debt, or if Dennis had really managed to dupe Eddie too.

I have since noticed that although Dennis was on the Brown Capital Management Board of Trustees, he has been removed from their website. In many of Dennis' public documents online, he has removed Brown Capital from his work history.

Eddie's loans were only the tip of the iceberg that I was unraveling. Where indeed had the money to pay his bills come from?

Stephen Kaufman loaned Dennis $100,000 in December 2009 and another $150,000 the following July. Richard Parsons, $125,000 in early 2010. Jim Cash made three loans to him between June and September 2010 totaling $135,000. A. Barry Rand loaned him $25,000 in May 2011 and then made a second loan. The list went on.

Jim Cash, a former professor at Harvard Business School, had issued him two $50,000 loans and one for $35,000 while Dennis was still a part of the Obama Administration.

Cash had served on the boards of Microsoft, General Electric, Chubb Corporation, Walmart and Veracode.

These were powerful men and relatively large sums of money. What, if anything, had they expected to gain from loaning the Deputy Secretary of Commerce the money to bankroll his lifestyle? What perks could he promise them from inside his office on Constitution Avenue?

Richard Parsons is a business titan and a master negotiator. As a former CEO of Citigroup and AOL Time Warner, he knows what he is doing and he understands the rules of the game. Not just anyone gets a seat at his table.

It was common knowledge that you don't get a seat at his table unless you are bringing something to it, at least according to my personal experience.

"I always knew I would rise to the top," he is quoted as saying. "It never occurred to me that I couldn't."

That could have been Dennis' motto, too.

Dennis asked Dick Parsons for an approximately $125,000 loan in January 2010. He agreed, and wiring instructions were exchanged. Simple as that. His loan to Dennis was the only one that would be paid back with interest as far as the paper trail reveals.

When I tried to contact Dick Parsons to get his deposition, it was as though he evaporated into thin air. He was untouchable.

Wulf von Schimmelman, the former chairman of Deutsche Postbank AG, served on the board of Accenture with Dennis and had loaned him upwards of $30,000.

I remember one time when we went to Paris for an Accenture board meeting and we were on a yacht on the Seine. It was a beautiful day, but Dennis kept getting flustered that I was talking to his fellow Board members, including Wulf von Schimmelman. I had no idea why he was so upset. Had he expected me to be silent and wait for him to do the talking? Maybe he did not like that I was comfortable speaking for myself. Had he wanted me to seem more impressed with his life of luxury?

A. Barry Rand had issued Dennis two separate $25,000 loans. Rand was the first African-American CEO of AARP and an active supporter of the Affordable Healthcare Act, otherwise known as Obamacare. He had served as chairman and CEO of Avis Group Holdings; CEO of Equitant Ltd.; and executive vice president, Worldwide Operations at Xerox Corporation; and was on numerous other boards and chairman of the Board of Trustees of Howard University.

Rand also had an estate in Stamford, but refused to be a deposed in Connecticut, forcing me to take his deposition in Washington, D.C. instead. At the time, sitting at the helm of one of the most powerful lobbying forces in the United States, he thought he was above the law. Many of them did.

He was frequently rude to my attorney, self-important and arrogant. He tried to evade receiving subpoenas and eventually was sanctioned and ordered to pay for my attorney fees and sit for a deposition. When he or his wife finally sent me a check as ordered to cover attorney fees, there was a condescending note attached: "I hope this helps."

Stephen P. Kaufman, another Harvard Business School lecturer and CEO of Arrow Electronics, had issued Dennis a $100,000 loan and a $150,000 loan over the course of a few months. Dennis had pushed back on repaying the loans, first in May 2010, then December 2010, and again in June 2011. Each time he promised that conditions would improve and he would somehow scrape together the payments.

Power is a strange thing. The promise of power is even stranger. Just by cashing the check without any tangible promise, in my eyes, it was as though Dennis was being bought, bit by bit and piece by piece, until he was gone and in his place was a man who belonged to the crowd.

It was as though they were buying and selling shares in one another's success. Debts that they would have to eventually collect.

Power begets power. That much is a fact. I had been impressed by Dennis' Board positions when we had met. I believed that he and his colleagues were good people. I was naïve enough to believe that being named to these positions meant they were among the best of the best. I never estimated that these powerful men could be in it for anything but honest reasons.

So many people were invested in Dennis. Investing their own dollars, their own names to support his myth. It is no wonder he became so angry when he realized that the illusion was shattering.

When do you lose your power?

Maybe when you lose your followers.

It was not just Dennis' wealthy friends who were waiting for payments from him — he had developed a history of simply not paying his bills.

We were hosting a charity dinner at Fleur D'Eau in April 2011. The limestone terrace around the house had cracked over the winter and needed $7,000 worth of repairs. Dennis made a few payments to the stone masons, but then he stopped. Months later, he still had not finished paying them.

We had commissioned a painting during our marriage. We knew the artist, Franco Accornero, through Brooke — she was friendly with his son and we had entertained Franco and his wife in the past.

Franco painted beautiful portraits, so I said to Dennis one day, "Wouldn't it be wonderful to have a painting to put over the fireplace at Fleur D'Eau?" Dennis agreed, and Franco quoted us $10,000.

Franco did not even ask for a deposit, and he completed the painting in three weeks. When he was ready to deliver it, Dennis started stalling. He asked Franco to make little changes and then began refusing to pay him.

Our painting sat waiting at the Accornero home, and they would call every so often seeking payment. People around town would see the painting at their house and tell me how much they loved it. I did too.

The situation quickly became embarrassing. I did not understand why Dennis was not paying Franco, and I'm sure Franco did not understand why he was not getting paid, especially while we were busy jetting off to Paris or wherever.

I sought Franco out after Dennis and I separated. I apologized for the way he had been treated and began paying him in installments. The last thing I wanted now was a painting of the two of us, but paying Franco for his work was the right thing to do.

"Why don't we paint him out?" Franco suggested one day as we pondered what do to with the portrait.

"Why don't you paint him out and paint Moe in!" my father suggested when I told him about the painting.

My father was a smart man.

So Franco added Moe, and I finally was able to pay him for the painting in full.

I too was far from immune from Dennis' financial machinations. He dropped my car insurance, stopped putting money in the joint account, cut off my Delta flight privileges against a court order, stopped paying the utilities without any warning and cut off my credit cards. I also was left to pay for regular upkeep around the estate while trying to pay off the many people Dennis had stiffed.

Loans were not the only means Dennis used to bankroll his lifestyle I realized as I uncovered yet another layer of discrepancies. As I started looking at board policies and perks, I found another source of income he was receiving if one chooses to be less than forthright. Dennis while serving on the board of Northwest Airlines, which merged with Delta Airlines, was entitled to free, first-class flights. This includes spouses and dependents.

Most of the other companies on Dennis' résumé reimbursed his travel expenses to their board meetings and conferences. With that, Dennis seemed to work out a way to manipulate the Delta perks to make them even more advantageous personally than the Delta policies stipulated, since the Delta policy clearly stated the benefits could not be used for business and/or financial gain.

First, Dennis would use his free Delta flights for business travel, and then he would request reimbursement from companies like Accenture for the flights. Sometimes he would receive thousands of dollars. As far as I could tell from his papers, the reimbursements were funneled right back into his living expenses. To illustrate this point, a first-class round-trip ticket to South Africa was valued at more than $10,000. A first-class round-trip ticket for two to Paris was more than $16,000. Accenture would reimburse Dennis for his airfare expenses. These numbers added up.

As it began to dawn on me what Dennis was doing, I asked our accountant, Robert S. Cook, CPA, if the airfare reimbursement was income. I also inquired as to whether or not it was tax fraud. Amazingly, he said "no." Shortly thereafter, he disengaged me and continued to represent only Dennis.

I did not know where to go with all my suspicions and information. It seemed like everyone I told was willing to turn a blind eye. Sometimes I truly felt like I was crazy and the rest of the world was perfectly content to excuse all of Dennis' lies and illegal behavior.

When it comes to lies inside a marriage, regardless whether it is infidelity or shady white-collar business practices, it is still personal and it hurts.

I thought back to the day we met for our prenup consultation in Westport. Dennis learned all my private circumstances without having to reveal a thing. By declining the prenup, he looked like Prince Charming.

If he had gone through with the prenup, he would have had a legal duty to disclose his financial status fully and accurately, and this was something Dennis could never have done. He had looked down on me for having debt, so how could he admit that he was living a complete lie?

Lies upon lies, and possibly years of getting others to loan him money and neglecting to pay them back. At the prenup meeting, he only had to throw out a high estimate of his net worth. He did not even have to show any records to back it up.

The compromise arrangement we reached instead of the prenup was fraught with loopholes as well. Dennis could change his estate documents at any time, and I later learned that he frequently disinherited and reinstated Denny and Dawn based on how he was feeling about them on any given day. Disinheriting a wife would be just as easy. Our agreement was not a long-term document for him, but simply a scorecard. What appeared to be a generous bequest could always be rewritten at a later date. Indeed, one of the first things Dennis did after we separated was rewrite his will.

And because I had conceded to his plan, he could make these moves without the consequences of breaching a prenup. In essence, I had little to no protection.

His sizable life insurance policy also could be decreased at any time. Dennis believed he could reduce his $3 million policy with its $100,000 annual cost quickly to a lower amount or cancel it outright.

After our separation, that is exactly what he tried to do. He had already reduced the insurance policy from $3 million to $1 million with my approval. Luckily, one of the few smart things I did when we got married was to get the life insurance policy in my name so I was the owner.

When Dennis threatened to cancel the policy, my attorney wrote to him and said that was extortion. Dennis had no standing to cancel the policy since he did not own it. Nevertheless, though he had promised to make the quarterly $5,240 premium payments, after we separated he simply refused. The court forced him to give me some money for expenses, but I had no other alternative but to pay the premiums myself during the ongoing divorce proceedings.

Dennis could not stop bragging about his compound in Guatemala from the day we met. While Denny was the one who lived there full time, Dennis claimed to maintain his own supposed wing and had always stated that it was his home, too. I learned that in November 2010, he told his "friends" that he had been trying to sell his Guatemala home for months and would be able to repay some of his debts once it sold.

Yet, at his divorce depositions, he denied having any stake at all in the property.

In the government financial disclosure Dennis had to file when the FBI was vetting him for the Commerce Department, he listed a home in La Antigua, Guatemala, with an estimated value of $650,000.

"My son lives in La Antigua, Guatemala," the disclosure form read. "And I'm the joint owner of the house there with him, where he resides."

Clearly that was the compound we had visited during our marriage. He purchased the property by sending funds to Denny, but still he claimed in divorce proceedings that he was not an owner, nor a joint-owner, nor did he have any sort of interest in the property.

Dennis became visibly frustrated when the Guatemala property came up at one of his depositions. He claimed FBI agents had told him to list the property even though he did not own it, because he had been sending funds to Guatemala to purchase it.

"It closed the loop," he said. But that was not true.

"I am not the owner of the home in Guatemala," he repeated time and again at the deposition, although it appeared plain and simple on the paper we put before him. "Any number of times I will say it, I do not own a home in Guatemala."

However, he later contradicted himself and stated that he owned the property jointly with Denny.

At some point, the compound was placed under an anonymous corporation. I saw documents showing $984,000 wired to Denny over the years, but I still could not make sense of exactly what they were doing. Where was the money going, and where was the tax record?

I could only conclude that I was still missing pieces of the puzzle — the money had to be somewhere. There were enough signs along the way that he was continuing to fund his lifestyle one way or another; he had just done a damn good job creating a sea of confusion, a fantasy of wealth under a web of deception leading back to…what, exactly? Was there an actual bank account he kept tucked out of sight? I do not know if I will ever find out.

Most likely, I also will never know how Dennis was able to maintain an American Express Centurion/Black Card up until at least 2014. Despite the 2012 foreclosure proceedings for the mansion and his 2013 bankruptcy filing, he still maintained a card that, as I understand, requires the holder to have stellar credit, income exceeding $800,000 a year, and more than $5 million in assets. Also, the cardholder must be able to pay the yearly fee of $2,500 just to have the card. I had to wonder was he using an alias or alternate Social Security number? Did American Express not check his credit? Maybe this was his way of maintaining his illusion of wealth on paper. Dennis met none of their requirements as far as I now knew.

CHAPTER 9

UNDER HIS POWER

Dennis was angry. Of course he was. Everything about our situation made him furious. All his cherished possessions were locked away and out of his control in a mansion in Connecticut with his second wife. His collections. His trophies. His files. His medals. His wine. His jade. Everything was trapped beyond his reach.

"Worst decision I ever made was to marry that woman!" he wrote in an email to one of his friends and lenders.

Not only had the Connecticut estate been a bad investment that had jeopardized his credibility with his buddies, now it was one large and looming symbol of failure. A fortress built on loss.

I was feeling trapped, too. I described some of Dennis' antics to our marriage counselor.

"He could be either a sociopath, a narcissist, or have borderline personality disorder," our counselor told me. "There are a lot of guys like that in the CIA."

Dennis told me he had learned strategy and spycraft during his days at Army College and as an intelligence officer. Later on, he told me he had been involved in espionage during his time in Southeast Asia and that he was a spy handler for the CIA, although he was never clear about his full involvement.

With Dennis, it was often hard to separate fact from fiction.

When he talked about his time at Disney, he spun elaborate stories of entertaining European royalty, wining and dining and jetting about Europe at the helm of Disney Consumer Products for Europe, the Middle East and Africa. But he also described the darker undercurrent. He had been part of a program in which people would conduct espionage under the cover of a large corporation. It was a world I never knew existed.

I nodded as I thought about what the counselor was saying. I had started reading about possible mental health diagnoses during the dark months when I had assumed Dennis was depressed. Now things were beginning to make sense. What had happened was not so much a betrayal as a characteristic deeply engrained in Dennis. He had not snapped at all; he had revealed himself to me, his true self, for the very first time.

Now he was using his so-called CIA tactics: deny, deflect, delay.

"The best thing you can do," the counselor continued, "is don't engage."

Do not feed the beast. I knew I was going to have to cling to those words to get through the days, weeks and years that followed. Dennis was a formidable opponent, and I knew he would take me down easily if I did not hold strong.

Men like Dennis are cunning. They approach divorce just as they would a business transaction, and they do not expect their wives to challenge them. By proceeding rationally, they are ahead of the curve — steps ahead. They expect the playing field to be in their favor, and they do not fight fair.

I was in a battle with Dennis to try to regain my financial stability and maintain my mental and physical wellbeing. Dennis referred to it as a war of attrition.

Dennis' biggest mistake was leaving his documents behind at Fleur D'Eau. Because of that one misstep, I had a decent chance of discovering what was really going on under the veneer that glossed over his life.

The discovery process can be an overwhelming time in any divorce — asking the other party to produce documents and presenting them with questions and statements to build an accurate financial picture. With Dennis, I was learning that the truth would not always be easy to find. The layers went on and on.

The process includes depositions given under oath and penalty of perjury, and document production for financial and other records that can be used in court.

In our case, my attorneys were not only going to take Dennis' deposition. They wanted to depose each of his lenders to learn their role in Dennis' grand games. I was able to take depositions of Eddie Brown in Maryland, A. Barry Rand in Washington, D.C. and Stephen Kaufman in Massachusetts.

None of the information came easily, and I paid tens of thousands of dollars in legal fees and costs to bring Dennis to justice. My professional experiences had prepared me for this moment, but the personal cost was substantial.

When I came face-to-face with Dennis at his first deposition, I remembered our counselor's words. I would not engage, I would not show weakness, but I did want to ask him one question: "Where are your teeth?"

I knew it was mean, but it was too big to ignore. I could see that he had been having some serious dental problems, and his teeth were a mess.

I had a difficult time recognizing the man sitting across the room — the man fumbling with his glasses as he attempted to talk his way out of his lies, skirt the issues, explain away the evidence, deny everything — was the same person that I had married: the chivalrous, learned man, the groom in the crisp white suit, the man addressing members of the United States Senate at his confirmation hearing, so poised and well-spoken that I could not help but feel butterflies when he talked.

I did not want to believe that these two men were both my husband. This was the same person who read to me from his treasured first edition of *Lord Chesterfield's Letters* and passed himself off as a beacon of morality and wisdom.

Only he wasn't. He was far from it. I would not want to go on a date with someone like that, let alone marry him, love him, expect to start a family with him.

The illusion had fallen away, and what was left was an old man with bad teeth — a low-life and a bully. Vicious and cruel. His deposition was an ugly window into his thoughts.

He claimed he had spent all of his money on me.

I thought he had been unfaithful during a trip to Singapore because of symptoms I experienced shortly after his return. Dennis tried to explain it away by stating that we sometimes had vaginal and anal sex without cleaning up in between. I was absolutely mortified. I had never once had anal sex in my previous relationships. I did it because I had trusted Dennis and went along with his request. To have these graphic and inaccurate descriptions of our sex life used against me during a deposition was almost more than I could bear. I felt violated by his words, just as he had intended.

After all of that, I later learned he had not even gone to Singapore in the first place. The souvenir he allegedly brought back from his trip was just some trinket he bought in the U.S. Lies! Always lies!

He bragged about being politically connected and how President Obama lauded his service during his year as Deputy Secretary of Commerce; that former Secretary of Commerce Gary Locke said everything he touched was better than it was before he got involved. At his advanced age and with his considerable work experience, he said, it was more fitting for him now to mentor young businessmen than to earn money himself.

With regard to his debts? "At this stage, I'm a realist," he said. "At this age, there is no way possible, unless I hit the lottery, that I'm going to ever have anywhere near the money to repay any of these people."

He said he was glad fertility treatments had failed, because there was a history of mental illness in my family.

How far we had fallen to get to this awful place.

"He said that he took his pistol down to the pond while I was in California and considered taking his own life," I told the marriage counselor, my voice quiet and fearful. I remembered feeling that something was not right that day.

"That never happened Dori," he said plainly. "Think about it. You know that's a lie."

"How do you know that?" I asked.

"Narcissists don't commit suicide. They hurt other people, but they don't hurt themselves," he replied.

"Then why would he say it?"

"He will say anything right now to get your sympathy so that he can continue to manipulate you."

Dennis liked to watch spy movies. He was fascinated with espionage — be it his supposed real life experiences or a Hollywood action film.

By the time I met him, I think his knowledge of strategy and stealth affected the way he handled himself at all times. His smooth talking and brilliant oratory skills were straight out of a Tom Clancy novel. The very thing that had attracted me to him on our early dates revealed a much more sinister streak. He knew what he needed to say to get his way, and he rarely faltered.

I noticed through every rough patch in our relationship that Dennis liked to play mind games. What's more, he was very good at them. He could get inside my head. He knew precisely how to tap into his opponent's insecurities to knock them off balance and blindside them so he could have the upper hand.

Dennis' self-proclaimed spy training seemed to re-enforce his belief that he never had to answer to the same consequences as everyone else or conform to anyone else's rules. Or at least, that is the way he acted, like he was somehow better, chosen, special.

In order to survive, I would have to think steps ahead. I would have to start thinking like Dennis — anticipating his next move so he would never be able to lure me into his games again.

It was a Tuesday, and I was supposed to be on my way to D.C. to see our marriage counselor. I was sitting in the backyard behind Fleur D'Eau, getting some sun and breathing in the clean autumn air, when I heard Moe barking.

"Hello?" I called as I walked back towards the house. "Is someone there?"

As I stepped inside and rounded the corner, I spotted Dennis frantically packing, moving from his study, from room to room.

"I did not know you were coming. Why didn't you call?" I asked.

He was silent. He did not say a word as he continued rummaging through his closet, loading his black rental SUV down with everything he could carry out the door. He never disclosed the items and the jade he took that day on his bankruptcy paperwork.

"You cannot do that!" I said. It was clear he had not expected me to be home — had he planned to clear the place out before I noticed he had been in the house?

"I am calling the police," I warned him. "You had better get going."

Dennis went to the police station that day too; he wanted to report that some of his things were missing, threatening legal action if I would not tell him what had happened to his precious jade.

Years later, I found a receipt for a piece of furniture with a hidden compartment. I recognized it immediately as a piece that was still in his study. I found the hidden compartment. It was empty. But I also remembered that Dennis had gone straight to his study that day when he came to raid the house.

He knew I never went into his study. What had been so important that he needed an extra level of safekeeping? I will probably never know.

The police flagged our home for potential domestic violence that day. They told Dennis to stay away, that he did not want this sort of conflict on the books. They told me that the only way to legally prevent him from taking things from our home was to file for divorce.

When the divorce papers arrived in his email a few days later, Dennis was angry that he did not get to file first. How dare I beat him to the punch? He quickly reverted to a sulking child when he did not get his way.

I knew I needed to get the automatic orders that are legally trigged when a party files for divorce in Connecticut. Once the orders are in effect, he could not remove or sell anything from Fleur D'Eau except for normal and customary expenses and to get legal counsel. At the time, I did not have enough money for a lawyer and I did not want to represent myself. Still, I went ahead and filed and then began trying to get counsel.

Dennis had our housekeeper, Maria, call me to try to get information. Just as she had been an uncomfortable bridge between Dennis and his first family, she found herself once again trapped in the middle of one of Dennis' domestic feuds.

He knew how to manipulate her, too.

I had asked Maria once, sitting at the kitchen island while she stirred a pot on the stove, about Dennis' relationship with his daughter and she replied simply in Spanish that they did not speak because he was "mentiroso" — a liar.

The Mouse

Dennis' time at Disney loomed large over Fleur D'Eau. We had posters and exclusive merchandise from the blockbusters that were featured during his tenure at the company in the 1990s: *The Lion King* and *Beauty and the Beast,* among others. An original sketch of Goofy as a samurai, signed for Dennis, was featured in our powder room.

I assumed Dennis was proud of his time at Disney. As always, I later learned there was more to the story.

Dennis never told me he was fired from Disney. He claimed he left of his own accord. He was always going to retire at fifty-five, and they offered him a pretty package to do so.

Pulitzer Prize-winning journalist James B. Stewart paints a very different picture of the animation empire in his book *DisneyWar*, including stories about Dennis that prompted an old friend to ask me about it after he finished reading the book.

I did not know anything about it and ordered a copy.

Dennis' role in *DisneyWar* is that of a side character, introduced as CEO Michael Eisner's "impetuous personnel decision." In fact, his first mention, which regarded his promotion to head of Disney's television division, included negative responses from his colleagues. "That's the most ridiculous thing I have ever heard," Stewart quoted one company official, and "Not even Michael could make a mistake that big," stated another.

The naysayers proved correct, as Stewart documented, and Dennis was on the way to being pushed out just months after his promotion: "Eisner had been hearing a stream of complaints. Hightower had become an embarrassment to him, and Eisner did his best to ignore him."

Of course, the company downplayed his departure as an early retirement in press releases.

I could not help but wonder just how many times Dennis had chosen an early exit in his career and whether this same story had played out in the Department of Commerce as it did in our marriage.

"What kind of a wife was she?" he had said to his giggling companion after he butt-dialed me.

What kind of a wife was I?

My husband was like a god to me. I believed whatever he said had to be true. I followed him smiling blind until the butt dial call. It is not that I did not know any better. I was not naïve but smitten — quite simply on autopilot.

Powerful partners with an agenda can do that to their spouses, transporting them to a state of complete and total trust where they are simply floating around inside the other spouses's world. It's not that the spouses are not bright; it is that they have been programmed not to think, never to question, but merely to exist. I see it all the time in my practice. These partners exist solely as objects, and most people don't expect them to be anything more.

It is disturbing to me. When marriages fail, it is almost always one partner or the other who is thought to be more knowledgeable about the financial and legal processes. That partner knows how to hide things and how to get what he or she wants. They have learned how to control and manipulate, and they can starve their partners for resources until they are desperate.

Dennis tried this too. He stopped paying the utility bills, stopped all regular maintenance on the home we shared. He cut me off from the credit cards, flight benefits and bank accounts, and he lowered his income. He stopped making the mortgage payments and, predictably, Fleur D'Eau went into foreclosure.

It is a common maneuver. One spouse decides to squeeze the other out, causing enough panic to force a compromise. Starve the autopilot partner long enough, and you win by default because they do not know what else to do. They give in because they run out of options.

A spouse can lose their power when they are on autopilot, and suddenly, the game is over and the other spouse has won before they even realize they were playing a game.

In most ways, Denia was a much better Washington, D.C. wife than I ever could have been. She appreciated the lifestyle: the clothes, the jewelry, the vacations, the prestige of standing by his side at the opera or the ball.

She could accept all the baggage of being Mrs. Dennis F. Hightower and just smile through it.

I felt for Denia. When I first looked her in the eye in that shabby little kitchen in Guatemala, I could not possibly have understood the depth of her pain. After forty-two years of marriage, Dennis had destroyed her, too.

Maria told me Denia sometimes would ask her about him.

"Why doesn't she just move on with her life?" Dennis used to say.

It was not that simple. I realized that then, but I know it even better now. She was in her sixties when her marriage fell apart. After living in an 18,000-square-foot home with an indoor pool, she found herself in an apartment with many of her possessions in storage. According to Dennis, his daughter Dawn held that against him. She saw all the devastation up close. She saw how that marriage disintegrated and she was not about to forgive and forget.

When Denny learned that Dennis and I had separated, he warned me. "He tried to screw my mother out of a lot. Be careful," he said. "I've seen this behavior from Dad before."

Dennis was so quick to dismiss his first wife. Although I had accepted his stories about the cause of their marital breakdown, I think I always knew there was more to the story.

Moving

Even Dennis' lengthy résumé started to take on a new appearance when held up against the man lurking behind the mask.

He knew how to carry on at first; how to get in the door and charm his new associates. But eventually, his lies became unsustainable. He could feel them slipping and spiraling, and he had to do anything he could not to get caught.

The easiest way to do that was to keep moving — spend two years here, two years there. Denia moved with him no fewer than nineteen times in their forty-two-year marriage: Ohio, Mexico, Washington, D.C., California and Paris. He was constantly moving, getting out before anyone could catch on. Getting out before anyone became the wiser, before it could all come tumbling down.

While he was moving up, he was also moving away.

CHAPTER 10

SALVAGING MYSELF

Dennis had hoped filing for bankruptcy would wipe his slate clean. Not only would his debts be discharged, he assumed I would not challenge the veracity of his filings. He was wrong again. Dennis failed to accurately disclose his assets to the Bankruptcy Court, and the entire process would prolong our divorce for years. If the Bankruptcy Court discovers fraud in the filing, this can prolong the bankruptcy, result in a denial of the discharge and subject the bankruptcy debtor to fines and even incarceration.

As the weeks and months and years passed, we had divorce, foreclosure and bankruptcy litigation all happening at the same time. I was hemorrhaging money on legal fees. We were losing Fleur D'Eau, and I was realizing that Dennis never expected me to question his actions. He expected to walk away from our life together unscathed.

When my marriage fell apart, I found myself adrift again. Two years wiser, I knew this time that no one was going to swoop in to save me. I did not want to be rescued anyway — that is not the way life works. I took a deep breath, swallowing my pride in one great gulp as I picked up the phone.

"Lisa, it's me," I said, my voice catching and cracking. "I'm so sorry. Dennis is gone. He left me with nothing. I need to get back to work."

Looking back, it was clear that Dennis needed to isolate me from the people in my life who were the most likely to speak up and ask questions — the people who might see through his charade and speak loudly enough to tip me off.

Despite being impressed with Dennis when she had first met him and introduced us, I think Lisa had figured him out early on. She had warned me to negotiate, to protect my finances, to use my power while I had it, before it all turned to dust. I would have advised a friend or a client to do exactly the same.

Once Dennis had pushed Lisa out of the equation, convinced me that I should not talk to her anymore, her fears were confirmed. She knew exactly what was happening, but it was too late.

"You can never trust these men," Lisa said.

I knew I had hurt her deeply, but there was no judgment in her voice that day, only a complete willingness to help me pick up the pieces. "Now, getting you back to work. Where can we start?"

Lisa is very smart and strategic. She has to be. What we do in these high-net-worth cases is help men and women get out of toxic relationships. For me to be a woman who had counseled and represented these husbands and wives, and yet was completely taken in by Dennis — in my second marriage, no less — it is regrettable, yes, but all too common. It confirms in my mind that no one is immune. I see deception all the time in court, but that was not enough to protect me in my own relationship.

I work to protect my clients every day. I try to take care of them and safeguard their interests. Yet, I had failed to protect myself.

I was embarrassed, as someone who was raised to be strong and self-sufficient, to admit I ever thought that way about a man, but I did. I was in love.

I was so busy propping up his life, creating a world to suit his needs and becoming the precise brand of wife that he wanted, that I neglected to take care of myself.

I knew I did not have a lot of time to protect myself after I filed for divorce. I had to take steps to protect myself, and I had to do it fast. At this point, I honestly did not know to what lengths Dennis would reach, but I knew he was angry. Whatever he was planning next, I was not going to be a victim and intended to protect my legal rights.

Soon after I filed for divorce, I started noticing things happening around the property at Fleur D'Eau. Things would suddenly break. The heating system in the guesthouse was disconnected and the locks to gates were broken.

I had never gotten so many flat tires or had so many acts of vandalism occur on the property. Suspicious? Definitely!

Over four years since I had filed for the divorce, I noticed one night that someone was outside, a car circling the driveway shortly after dark. I finally snapped; and stupidly, I ran up to the car.

"Get off my property!" I yelled.

It was not the smart thing to do, but I was tired of living like this. Tired of never feeling safe. Logically, I know I should have kept my cool, called the police immediately, tried to get the license plate number, but I was too traumatized to think clearly.

During a deposition, Dennis' attorney asked if a car with a specific license plate had come to the house. Fleur D'Eau sits so far back from the road that anyone inside would never see the license plate of a car parked outside. It is unlikely anyone would know that unless they were on a reconnaissance mission at the property.

This was Dennis' M.O. — destabilize me through small maneuvers and keep me just enough off balance until I would concede to his terms.

Finally we were able to confirm that he had been playing his spy games once again. I got a copy of the surveillance report and the court ordered Dennis to stop the surveillance and pay my attorney fees. He continued to deny having anything to do with it, of course. I found it interesting that he had the means to pay a private investigator.

Wolves

Every creak in a floorboard or rustle of the trees outside my bedroom window caused my heart to race. I felt short of breath whenever Moe barked and nothing seemed to be there, preparing myself for what I would do if there ever were an intruder.

I had read about a fellow lawyer in Connecticut who had disappeared and was murdered. Suddenly I found myself paying more attention to stories in the newspaper and on the news; the ones with terrible, tragic endings that we never think could happen to us.

Now the ghost of Dennis seemed to haunt Fleur D'Eau. I constantly felt I was being watched. I would pause in the hall and see the burnt flicker of something in the corner of my eye: was it a light bulb? A camera flash? Nothing at all? I was living in a constant state of hyper-vigilance. Maybe it was a side effect of training my brain to think like Dennis, to anticipate his plots and lies.

I now inhabited a world where princes did not always look like princes and villains did not always look like villains. Either of the two could transform at any moment.

Who could I trust?

Dennis had once told me that he would kill me if I was with another man. The words had fallen out of his mouth as we stood in the foyer of Fleur D'Eau. Then, after thinking it over for a moment, he corrected himself — "No," he said. "I'd have someone else kill you."

I stared up at my bedroom ceiling, praying that this would be the night I could sleep; that for just one second, I could close my eyes, forget his words, and calm my racing heart. I did not want to believe Dennis was capable of hurting me.

But a part of me could not shake the gut feeling that he was capable of anything.

"I have your documents. I have them in a safe place and other people have them too," I said calmly to Dennis at my deposition, as I had been advised to do by the police.

I needed to let Dennis know that other people had his records. I was not keeping quiet and I was not the only one who knew about his situation.

It sounds paranoid when I put it into words, but I knew how he operated. I worried what might happen if he thought I was the only one who knew about the things I had found, if I was the only one with the full picture and the only one who could expose him. I was afraid that he might hire a hit man to take me out. He had already threatened to kill me if I was with another man. He said he wouldn't do it himself; he would have someone else do it. Looking at my marriage objectively, it would not have come as a surprise. Nothing would have surprised me in those days.

My father's family comes from Harlem, gritty people who know how to dig in and protect themselves. I may have grown up privileged, the girl in suburbia who goes to horseback riding camp and takes ballet lessons, but I always heard stories about where my father had come from, my roots.

My father was one of eight children. He had lost his own father when he was young, and his family moved around a lot. My father attending City College and then Columbia. He may have left the neighborhood and gotten an education, but that true grit does not disappear ever.

Now was the time to flip the switch and turn it on.

I had to make sure I was not going to disappear. Too often, when you're afraid of someone like this, the instinct is to retreat from the world. It would have been far easier for me to be afraid, to hide and continue to wallow inside the house and simply hope that he would feel he had done enough damage and leave me alone. Unfortunately, that's not how the world works. That was not the way to protect myself. That was the way to become a victim.

I knew I had to do exactly the opposite. The best way to protect myself was to get back out into the public eye, and fast.

I met Helen, a local publicist, one day when I was getting my nails done. We clicked instantly and went to work rebuilding my name professionally. I was quickly transforming from a weak and broken political wife into a strong attorney once again.

In time, Helen also would become a close friend and confidante, bonding over our little dogs and the ups and downs of the most turbulent years of both our lives.

While being married to Dennis is not a line on my résumé, it is an experience that enlightens how I work every day. Living through hell changes everything.

Because of Dennis, I understand wealth on a different level. I represent men and women whose spouses are business tycoons, of high net worth and/or have equally impressive titles. The moneyed spouse usually starts out with the upper hand because their resources allow them to play games; but thanks to Dennis, I am aware of many of the games that can be played. I appreciate from a different perspective that financial disclosures in a divorce may not be complete. I know I have to read between the lines to find the gaps.

Nowadays, I go into new cases knowing I can never take documents at face value. I remember Dennis' phony appraisal forms and divorce decree. It goes against everything we have been taught, but just because something is in writing does not always mean it is real. I have to look closer and I have to question everything. You do not always have all of the information, and they will not just hand it to you, but you can always raise questions. Sometimes a single question is all it takes to introduce that tiny bit of doubt that causes an illusion to come crashing down and ultimately shatter.

My professional life was finally starting to get back on track again. In fact, I felt as though I was actually coming into my own and becoming the attorney I wanted to be. *The Connecticut Law Tribune* named me Solo Practitioner of the Year in 2014, and I stood, once again smiling for the camera. But this time, I did it entirely on my own terms. I was in charge of my own life again, and I did not have to be picture perfect anymore.

My confidence had been so rattled, my sense of self so completely destroyed during my marriage to Dennis, that I surprised myself time and again. The pieces were falling back into place, and I liked the woman reflected in the mirror once again.

I never could have predicted that the divorce case Lisa recommended me for when I reached out to her would turn out to be one of the top cases in Connecticut and by far the longest case I had ever had. For years, I was on a journey with the same client through ups and downs and appeal after appeal. As her story unfolded, I found my own path again.

When you rebuild from a toxic relationship, you are building yourself back from a foundation that has been badly damaged. I have even more compassion for my clients now that I have lived through this too.

Some people can just move on from a bad marriage, but that is harder to do when you are forty-five or fifty years old, and harder still when the life you knew turns out to be a complete and utter lie. There are so many people in this age group that have been conned by parties they loved, men they expected would love them for the rest of their lives.

Remembering Dennis' empty promise inside a birthday card, I bought myself my own Cartier watch when a girlfriend and I went to a jewelry show in Tucson. It was deeply discounted, absolutely beautiful, and not made of paper.

I am careful about the people I trust these days, more cautious than ever before, and I do not think that will ever change. I found ways to learn how to truly be alone and rely on myself once again. I took ballet classes at Broadway Dance and Pilates at the Alvin Ailey Extension in New York City. Both forced me to reconnect with myself — slow down and rediscover my balance and my love of dance.

I saw *Sex and the City 2* and decided to go to Dubai. Why not go on an adventure of my own? I always wanted to visit the Middle East and I was intrigued when Dennis talked about his own trips. It took the *Sex and the City* girls to finally convince me — I was just going to go for it.

Slowly, I was learning how to take care of myself again and this time, I did not have to skimp to pay tuition and make ends meet. I would be smart; I would buy St. John, but wait until off-season when it was marked down. Yet, this wave of security, also, would be short-lived.

Travel was restorative and I promised myself to do more of it.

The morning mist was just clearing off the California mountains and the sun broke through, illuminating the vistas and warming my face. I paused to breathe in the morning air.

The divorce had been a shock to my system, not only mentally, but also physically. My blood sugar started climbing and I was now prediabetic. Diabetes runs in my family and I watched both my father and my grandmother struggle to keep it under control. I had gestational diabetes when I was pregnant with Brooke and began experiencing premature labor just five-and-a-half months into my pregnancy. I knew the diabetes might return and sure enough, just as my marriage fell apart, I began experiencing health problems. I knew I had to start taking care of myself if I wanted to be healthy. I could not do that with Dennis looming over my life so I made plans to attend a premier fitness retreat at The Ranch in Malibu for a few days.

I wanted to do something outside my comfort zone and this fit the bill perfectly. I am used to taking walks with my girlfriends, but people at The Ranch hike real mountains and workout hard for hours every day. I was growing as both a person and an athlete as I pushed myself to keep up and keep going, to continue moving up the mountain even when my legs were tired and my body ached.

During my time at The Ranch, I even learned how to cook a few dishes. My mother could not believe it.

Staring down over the bluff, my mind drifted back to Connecticut, and I thought about what I would face when I went home. I was comfortable with the idea of being alone.

I'm an independent soul — self-contained and controlled. I do not remember ever being any different. My older sister had mental health issues while we were growing up. As time went on, I became increasingly independent and self-contained as my parents had to focus their attention on her.

I never cared about school as much as my sister did. I was not a star student; I did not care if I got an A or a D. School was never my passion or focus. I always had dance. I studied ballet, but I did not have a ballerina body. Even at my thinnest I had curves, so I switched gears and discovered modern dance.

Sometimes I wonder why I went into law.

I thought I would be helping people and fighting to make things fair, but the truth is that law is divisive and difficult — family law in particular. Two parties can come into the divorce process wanting a fair agreement, wishing to keep things civil, but the very nature of the process pits them against one another as staunch opponents.

Readjusting my expectations, my definition of fairness is the most difficult part of my work. The part I had never really bargained on back in the beginning.

Yes, outwardly I may seem self-contained and reserved. Oh, but underneath, I'm fiercely protective of my family, and I have never backed away from taking care of myself and the people I love.

I was furious that Dennis had taken loans from my mother back in 2011. Nothing could have pissed me off more. My mother had first gotten pulled into Dennis' mess when he could not make a life insurance payment and then, when another emergency inevitably came up, she loaned him more money for a mortgage payment.

I asked him a couple times, in writing, when he was going to repay my mother. I knew we needed a paper trail to make sure she got paid. I did not want to believe it, but from his track record I knew she might never see her money.

As I had feared, he never even tried to pay my mother back, not a single cent. He still owes her more than $34,000 plus attorney's fees and other expenses she incurred while trying to get her money back.

I exhaled deeply, feeling that inner strength that would get me through the days and months that followed. I stretched my tired legs and started back down the mountain.

CHAPTER 11
TURNING THE PAGE

It was a bitterly cold day in February and my mind was a blur as I got ready in the dressing room off the master bedroom. I worried about the ongoing divorce, Dennis' bankruptcy, the looming foreclosure, where I would go next and how I would handle the move. I was in the midst of lean times at work — I had just wrapped up a large case but had not been paid yet. I still did not have time to begin marketing my business. My mental to-do lists were growing longer by the second, and I was struggling with all the details.

Then everything came to a crash.

A car had driven straight into the front door. It went over the curb and through the stone garden wall and straight into the house. The door and walls had exploded clear into the foyer. The window of the dressing room where I was standing cracked.

The impact could be heard all the way up in my office at the opposite end of the house. My assistant was working up there that day and later told me that at first she thought a bomb had gone off. The impact sounded like an explosion. I was screaming to her to call 911 as I raced out to see my mother's car smashed into the side of the house.

She was hysterical, stuck behind the airbag in the driver's seat. Miraculously, the car was still running. I ran in my high heels to get a knife to puncture the exploded airbags so I could get her out of the car.

"Don't try to move, Mom," I yelled to her as I worked to cut through the airbag to deflate it and set her free. I was shaking as I reassured her. "You're going to be okay."

Of course, I had no idea in those first few minutes if this was true.

I called Helen: "My mother's been in an accident. Come."

She arrived ten minutes later expecting to drive me to my parent's home, not to see a wreck right there at my front door. By that time the police department, fire department and an ambulance team had all arrived, and their vehicles surrounded the top of the driveway. The medics had loaded my mother into the ambulance. She was bruised and sore, but, miraculously, she was not badly hurt. They continued to reassure me that she was doing okay.

She did not know how the accident had happened, but felt as though the car had almost accelerated on its own. I knew Dennis' team would try to twist it around to assert that we had purposefully damaged the property. I could already hear them.

The foreclosure finally was moving forward, and the property title on Fleur D'Eau was set to transfer the following day. My mother had come up to discuss our next steps in a conference call with her attorney for the money that Dennis still owed her. We planned to file a lawsuit to try to recover the $34,000 that she had loaned Dennis.

All roads led back to Dennis and our disaster of a marriage. I could not do it anymore; I could not lose one more thing to him. My mother easily could have been killed in that accident, and we both could have died had she crashed through the wall just a few feet from the door where I was standing.

It was game over. I had to get the hell out of that house. I was ready to leave this beautiful, awful, picture-perfect and wholly cursed place behind.

Fortunately, I had renewed our homeowners insurance despite knowing I could be off the property just weeks into 2016. My mother had car insurance, but the cost of repairs well exceeded its limits and my insurance had to pay the difference.

It is a tough lesson for a divorcing spouse: you always need to cover your ass. Taking a gamble is tempting when you are trying to save money to make ends meet and you are already paying steadily increasing legal fees and trying to make ends meet on your own. But, you never know what can happen in a fraction of a second. It is not worth the risk. My mother's accident is a perfect example of the collateral damage caused by Dennis to me and those who cared about me.

I had been looking for a new place to live for months, knowing I would need to rent something soon despite a timetable that was constantly up in the air. It seemed like every time I came close to an agreement, something would happen that prevented anything from moving forward.

Days after the accident, I signed a lease on a new home. It was as if something had shifted and now forward was my only direction. I had loved Fleur D'Eau, but it was not mine anymore. It never really was.

The landlord later confessed that, if not for my real estate agent and for Helen vouching for me, they never would have rented to me. Just thinking about it made me nauseous, but who could blame them? They had Googled my name and learned enough of my story to be wary. There is such an intense shame in losing your home. Add on having a bankruptcy that is not even my own attached to my name, and my credibility was suspect. The realtor commented: your husband should be in jail.

I felt pulled in a hundred directions in the days that followed. My reserves were already low, with little endurance to spread around. My mother was out of commission from her accident, and my father had been in the hospital recently with a heart condition. They still needed my help.

On top of that, Dennis was demanding to see every last one of his possessions. He claimed his property was at risk. I gave him access to everything he was looking to repurchase following the divorce and bankruptcy and all the other stuff. In addition to orchestrating my own move, I would have to finish unpacking and putting on display what remained of Dennis' life inside Fleur D'Eau so he could come by the estate for an inspection.

Helen was there with me practically around the clock, helping me pack up my home and deal with the mentally exhausting job of organizing Dennis' stuff. The piles and stuff never seemed to end, and I could not believe how much of it I had never even seen before. I had not always been there for the deliveries when we moved in, and his collections seemed to have multiplied in the storage rooms overnight. I devised a system and spent days preparing for him to arrive.

Honestly, I was just dreading being in the same room with him.

Dennis arrived in the morning in a police cruiser escorted by two police officers. They brought him around to the side of the house and into the dining room through the door to the back terrace. We had agreed that he would be allowed in the dining room, living room and the poolroom downstairs. That was it.

His possessions were all laid out across folding tables and on the floor, neatly displayed. My own items were packed in boxes that lined the opposite wall. Dennis slowly began pacing the dining room, looking over the tables. He looked confused, as if he expected his possessions to be exactly where he had left them. I think it surprised him that time had not stood still in his absence.

The officers realized almost immediately that Dennis and I needed to be kept apart. I quickly retreated into the kitchen and up to my home office as Helen took over with the officers.

"Are there any weapons in the house?" one of the officers asked her.

It was a good question. We had been sorting boxes in the downstairs storage room just days earlier when we found a box of bullets. To be honest, we were not entirely sure what they were until we found a pistol-cleaning kit packed away with them. I had not known they were there. We found out we could turn them over to the police and did exactly that.

According to Helen, Dennis' eyes were locked on his possessions as he started telling stories to the police officers — pointing out the expensive rugs he had purchased on a business trip to Turkey and his collection of watches from the Walt Disney Company. It was typical Dennis — weaving stories and trying to impress the officers.

How big a narcissist do you have to be to be schmoozing with the police while you are examining your non-possessions in the middle of a bankruptcy? He was practically caressing his jade, so happy to be reunited.

I stepped back into the room once or twice to answer questions, but otherwise I tried to stay busy packing up boxes in my office and finding things to do in the kitchen. With Dennis around, just breathing was difficult for me. Sometimes it seems as though he drains the very air out of the room.

Moe ran through the dining room and greeted Helen and the police officers, wagging his tail and circling ankles. He ignored Dennis completely. Animals just know.

For about for two hours Dennis looked through his possessions. He barely acknowledged Helen for over an hour, focusing only on the officers and his things. Finally, he decided to make a formal introduction.

"Hi, I'm Dennis Hightower," he said pompously, finally extending his hand.

"I know," Helen replied.

She told me later that she could not bring herself to shake his hand.

He showed her a picture of a small statue and told her that he needed to know where it was. She brought the picture to me in the kitchen. I had not seen that statue in years. It was the only item on his lengthy list of more than 200 items that we had not been able to locate inside that enormous house.

Dennis thanked her profusely for finding and organizing all of his possessions for him. Everything he demanded to see, from a large sofa to the smallest relic, she quickly found within his piles. Everything was inventoried and immaculate, and he knew it.

A letter arrived the following day, claiming everything was in disarray and he would be lowering his bid to buy back his property. What a liar.

"How can he be so cruel?" Helen asked me after he had left the property. "You did not deserve this."

I did not have an answer for her. She was right — he was cruel and self-absorbed. It was only about the stuff now. Nothing I had loved about Dennis was real. It was all my projection mixed up in his illusion.

Maybe I did not deserve this, but no one ever does. This is life. Shit happens and you just have to keep going. But it is so much easier said than done.

I had been weakened from years of psychological warfare. If I had not had people around me — Helen and Erin and Lisa and my parents— people who could shoulder the weight when I fell apart, I am sure I would have crumbled a long time ago.

There is no handbook for starting your life over again. Some days I cannot accomplish very much, and that is okay. When I watched the movie *The Martian,* I honestly could relate: Matt Damon's character may have been stranded on Mars, but I was stranded in my life. For both of us, it was about living one moment at a time, putting one foot in front of the other and dealing with one issue at a time.

Dennis insisted on using the same movers he had cheated out of money the last time they moved his files to store his possessions for the court during his bankruptcy. I do not know why they even agreed to work for him again. Prior to him engaging them, I had hired them to move me out of the house. He kept calling them, pestering them for the status of my move and details about what was happening at the house.

With the movers set to arrive on a Saturday, I spent the previous day driving back and forth, filling my car at Fleur D'Eau and unpacking it at my new home. The weather was freezing cold and the temperature continued to plummet throughout the day.

Helen drove back and forth in her own car, and together we moved my kitchen in its entirety. Before there was anything else in the new house, we had unpacked dishes and glasses into the kitchen cabinets and placed some pretty things around to make it look like a home.

I slowly unpacked my things into the bathroom, setting out my favorite soaps and lotions and makeup. I was methodically filling the empty canvas to make this look like the place where I belonged.

We were up until close to midnight unpacking at the new house. I had to hold onto the idea that this would be home, that winter would not last forever and I could be happy here.

Moving the bulk of my belongings to my new address took five full days. At one point, the temperatures dropped so unbearably low that the moving company could not get the truck started.

On the third day of the move, the area was hit with a bad ice storm and freezing rain. We continued our back and forth, packing and unpacking carloads, keeping pace with the movers to try to get everything cleared out as quickly as possible. A torrential rain arrived the fourth day, cleared away with a heavy snowfall, making for another miserable day of back and forth. It was all such terrible timing, one thing after another after another, that it was almost funny.

Through delayed moving trucks and frigid temperatures, bit by bit and box by box, I left behind Fleur D'Eau and everything it had represented to me for the last seven years.

I set up mail forwarding and loaded up the last stray items into my car to roll down the long driveway one last time. Our life together was in the rearview mirror and I was one step closer to being free.

The road to freedom involves many steps, however. More than four years later, our divorce case was still pending. Delays due to Dennis' bankruptcy filing, his failure to accurately disclose assets, my health challenges and other issues have caused the process to take far longer than anyone ever would have imagined.

I was flipping through a magazine in a waiting room when I stopped at a story about Teresa Giudice, the *Real Housewives of New Jersey* matriarch who had been sentenced to 15 months in a federal prison on fraud charges. I remembered that Helen had mentioned Teresa's case to me once, noting similarities between Teresa and Dennis.

The magazine article stayed in my head. Late that night, I was lying awake still thinking about it. Giving up on sleep, I got up and began to research her indictment. It was true, Teresa had been convicted of mail fraud, wire fraud and making false statements on loan applications — all things I believe Dennis had done.

He had made false statements on the loan applications for Fleur D'Eau. He had gone through Harbor Bank by way of Eddie Brown, misclassifying the property as commercial and not as a residence. He had taken out a mortgage through Emigrant Bank without disclosing the existing Harbor Bank loan. Both were made under false pretenses and with false information. He overstated his income. He overstated the value of his home in Washington, D.C., and also failed to disclose that he was only a partial owner of the house in D.C.

In bankruptcy court, he failed to disclose Guatemala as an asset, even though he had listed it on his government disclosure forms and said time and again that he would be able to pay off his debts once the property sold. Which was it? He also had failed to disclose his financial affairs accurately to the Bankruptcy Court.

Later, he would bid $75,000 to buy back his property after filing for bankruptcy. He could come up with that much money to buy back property, I thought, but he could not make any effort to pay back my mother or the dozens of other people he owed.

If they went after Teresa, why couldn't they go after Dennis? If I thought what he had been doing was illegal how could I possibly remain quiet?

Why should Teresa serve the time and Dennis get away with it all?

In my mind, the premise of the fraudulent avoidance action against Dennis is simple. First, he failed to list the Guatemala property on his Bankruptcy Asset Schedules. Second, Dennis sold the Guatemala property for a reasonably equivalent value and failed to account for the proceeds — depriving the bankruptcy estate of the asset. Third, Dennis, or someone on his behalf, fraudulently conveyed the Guatemala property for less than its reasonable equivalent value.

I brought the draft of the indictment to my attorney in December 2015, and held my breath as he paged through.

At the end of his full review, which took months, he drafted a letter to the Assistant United States Trustee, the United States Attorneys Office, the Executive Office for the U.S. Trustees Office of Criminal Enforcement and the United States Attorney, District of Connecticut. The letter contained a broad outline of Dennis' real estate-centric bankruptcy fraud, with copies of the documents that also supported the assertion that Dennis had committed acts of wire and mail fraud to procure certain debts — during and after his time in the Obama administration.

I spent hundreds of thousands of dollars in legal fees, and hundreds of hours of my own time pouring over documents. My resources are limited. It is now time for the government to take the lead and prosecute.

I have nothing to gain monetarily from an indictment — my lawyers have told me that time and again — but I still want this case to move forward. This is not only about money; it's about fairness and justice. I want Dennis to be held accountable for his actions. I owe that to myself, to my parents, to anybody who has been a victim of Dennis or might become a victim in the future of a man who thinks he is above the law.

Many times during our marriage, Dennis would tell me, seemingly out of the blue, "Dori, you're the most resilient person I've ever seen."

I did not think much of it at the time. I laughed and brushed it off as a funny sort of compliment, but it was a chilling warning in retrospect. Maybe he had known I was expendable from the very beginning. He had known all along that one day I would be left to pick up the pieces long after he had moved on.

I did not know I was capable. So many times I did not know if I could be strong enough to support myself — mentally, physically and financially — through this entire process. I did not know if I would ever put myself back together from the fragments Dennis left behind.

Spinning Gold

People often ask why I have kept the surname Hightower.

If I decide to keep Dennis' name, it will be because I see it as a badge of courage. I lived the past seven and a half years of my life and came out on the other side a different woman. I cannot be ashamed of my name and of the path I have taken. I took a chance on a new life and believed that life was handing me a fairy tale love story.

Marriages fall apart every day; people fail to live up to their promises; life is not tidy and no one gets through it unscathed. He may be a Hightower, but it is my name now, too.

My name, my brand, my story — not his

In the end, this was not a story about a man; it was about me growing into myself as a woman.

CHAPTER 12

THE POISON APPLE

"I don't believe in circumstances. The people who get on in this world are the people who get up and look for the circumstances they want, and if they can't find them, make them."

—George Bernard Shaw

Dennis lived by these words. He wrote them in a letter to Brooke on her 21st birthday, sharing with her the secrets to his greatness in a grandiose letter that read more like a business address than a birthday letter to his stepdaughter.

Make them.

That very same doctrine that allowed Dennis to enjoy a meteoric rise to success in business became the same sense of lawlessness that governed Dennis' circle.

There is a very fine line between "fake it till you make it" and fake it till you break yourself and others, even if you do not realize you are broken yourself.

These men and women of the Black Elite were a new world where a black man was now President of the United States — a world where they finally were able to rake in the power, a level of success that past generations of African-Americans had never dreamt possible. In this world, the Black Elite were free to make their own circumstances and play their own games.

That kind of power comes with a steep price.

In a way, they created success for one another. As a group they could prop one another up.

They possess a disturbing mindset of entitlement — a pervasive arrogance and a demeaning attitude toward people they believe are beneath their social class and status. They have the uncanny ability to think that rules and, in many instances, laws simply do not apply to them. They live in an exclusive bubble where they constantly feed each other's egos, discussing in pompous ways their wealth and material possessions. Yes, they think that they are smarter than other people and feed on a delusion that their so-called success is the result of a divine right.

This is a sad mindset, because it is devoid of important human qualities and values such as respect, sensitivity, compassion, empathy and love. Their unscrupulous behavior often results in irreparable harm and in distressing casualty to others, even their so-called loved ones.

Obama did not come up through the corporate ranks; he was never truly part of this Black Elite. He was more substantial than that. However, he was the ticket in for members of the Black Elite, or so they thought. So many people rallied around Obama, attempted to use him, viewed an opportunity to claw for control. In some ways, he was just as much of an outsider in their world as I was.

The job changed Obama. We all saw it playing out on our televisions during his first years in the White House. We saw him change before the cameras and the crowds. We watched as his hair quickly turned gray. He became learned about the ways of power, but instead of becoming absorbed into the elite world, he became wary and wise.

My marriage was only one small casualty in the game. Dennis' exit from the Obama administration another. I often wonder what they were covering up when they ceremoniously celebrated his departure with an event as only the powerful White House insiders can truly imagine. An honor, or a nice way to say, we do not want you here anymore, while saving face.

Why? Why do we let them do it? Why does no one call foul?

Maybe we let them play these games because we put them on a pedestal. I know I did. I began to idolize Dennis from the moment he smiled at me across the table at the London Hotel, his eyes so warm and kind. He was absolutely sure of his own greatness. Who was I to doubt?

We want to believe in their stories and sometimes, at our own peril, we want to believe in them.

The world loves a good story: fairy tales about men of principle, men of greatness, men who have climbed from nothing to transform their world and the pretty women who wave by their side. The insiders. The jet set. The power couples.

We ask those women who they are wearing and who does their hair, but not why they are standing so still and posed. There is a quiet fear brewing beneath those layers of makeup, a small voice asking, "Who is this person I married?" Their bodies are trembling with nerves under the weight of lies they sense but do not even know about. They are smiling blind.

And in the blink of an eye, the sparkle of an emerald, the flash of a camera, they have played us all.

Who will be the next great story?

EPILOGUE

It has been nearly six years since I filed for divorce from Dennis F. Hightower. It feels more like an entire lifetime.

Dennis has now admitted to putting false information on his government vetting documents and his loan applications, as well as covering up the proceeds from the sale of the Guatemala compound by transferring them to Denny. On May 16, 2017 Dennis' lawyer conceded that Dennis made a fraudulent conveyance to his son Denny of the Guatemala house. Rather than going to trial in the Bankruptcy case - a finding and judgment of a fraudulent conveyance has been made in the Bankruptcy court against both Dennis and his son Dennis F. Hightower, Jr.

Regarding our divorce case, a new Judge was appointed in 2016, after I filed a Judicial Grievance against the former Judge. It was clear that the proceedings before the then new Judge were problematic. Dennis would sit in the courtroom and laugh out loud while I testified. The judge let him carry on through my two days of testimony. Then all of a sudden, when evidence of his fraudulent activities was entered into evidence and he was asked to verify his signature on documents, Dennis stopped laughing.

On the third day of the trial, I went out for breakfast with Helen and her husband Richard after court was dismissed early. Helen decided to Google the Judge because she thought there was something familiar about her. As it turned out, the judge's former partner who is also her husband worked at a law firm I tried to retain shortly after filing for divorce. The lawyer I spoke to was a professional ethics specialist. He told me that they could not take my case because of a conflict of interest. This jogged my memory especially in light of our breakfast chat.

I somehow specifically recalled seeing the name of that same law firm written on a check that Dennis produced during the discovery process. It turned out that Dennis had consulted with the firm and the same exact lawyer to find out whether he could file a legal grievance against me with the Connecticut Statewide Grievance Committee.

Due to the potential conflict of interest created by the Judge's former law firm in which her husband still worked as a founding partner of the firm that at one time represented Dennis, I could not be too careful. Subsequently, my lawyer filed a motion to disqualify the judge presiding over my divorce trial and requested that she recuse herself. My motion for disqualification was granted and a mistrial was declared.

About five months later our new divorce trial was scheduled for March 2017. The new trial was moved to another courthouse in Connecticut – Middlesex. Shortly before the trial was scheduled to begin, in another twist, Dennis terminated his attorney, Catherine P. Whelan, or she quit and filed a notice to represent himself. Notwithstanding, the filing of his pro se Appearance in the case, Dennis refused to file any updated financial documents legally required for trial and ultimately failed to show up for his own divorce trial.

Dennis sent an ex parte letter to the Court – stating that his cancer has reappeared, his friends were dying and he was an old man. He stated in the letter, "I trust the Court to do whatever is honest and just under the circumstances . . . I have no spirit to spend in acrimony and contention what days are left to me on this Earth . . . In closing, I ask the Court not to treat my absence in any way as a sign of disrespect to the Court."

I went to court on the day set for that trial unsure what would transpire. A Judge requested we verify the information in the letter and contact Dennis. Since we did not have current contact information and there was no lawyer on the case, the only way I could think of to reach him was through a woman who had contacted me after she read the original Kindle version of this book. Why you may wonder did this woman who had met Dennis through a dating website- yes- the man who was too old to come to court for his divorce trial had been active on numerous dating websites and his dating partner contacted me. So we got his cell phone number from this dating partner and tried to contact him to no avail.

Since being contacted by dating partner number one, two other women have chosen to send me emails after reading the book. One had dated him, the other worked for him during his time at Disney. Never having written a letter like that myself, this truly made me wonder how many other women had been conned in his path.

On April 17 and 18th our divorce trial was finally adjudicated. I would be remiss if I did not include my Attorney Norm Pattis' closing argument in this final version of Smiling Blind.

ATTY. PATTIS: ... I'm always surprised when anybody asks me to appear in a family court case because it's not my area of expertise. That was pretty obvious to everybody here when the Court had to ask elementary jurisdictional questions.

But I'm always flattered and it's almost always either a high conflict case or a fellow member of the bar that does so. And I just cherish these opportunities and I'm grateful to Mrs. Hightower for putting her confidence in me.

The case has troubled me for the following reasons, they were together, briefly, and of course the brevity of the time they were together means that this was a brief marriage and therefore the consequences going forward ought not to be great.

But the consequences to Ms. Hightower, having chosen to believe this man in the context of a fairytale whirlwind – I was going to call it conquest, courtship, have been profound. She's no fool, she's a respected member of the bar, she tries matrimonial cases in a difficult and hotly contested forum in the Judicial District of Stamford. But she choose to believe that this man loved her when he took every pain, every effort to get to know her, studied her minutely, as you heard through Lisa's testimony yesterday, provided her not just with a car, a luxury car, when he realized she needed one and promised her, in effect, the world, taking her to the White House for dinner with Michele and Barack Obama. And gave her every reason to believe that her future would be glowing and glittering and she stood down some from her responsibilities and choose to respond, despite her reservations, to this overwhelming display of what she took, perhaps, mistakenly to be love. And I think we've all been foolish in love from time to time. And I think that she regrets the decision she made now.

But how was she to know it wasn't genuine? That the prince hadn't come to rescue the princess, in this case?

…he struggled financially and she struggled to honor the commitment she made to this man, if for no other reason than, in fact, that she's an honorable woman. And you've heard her say, in her testimony, from time to time, that she regards her obligation as an officer of the court seriously. And she has my utmost respect for that. Other people place their lives in her hands and the courts are entitled to rely upon our representations as factual and it's our obligation to speak the truth as we know the truth. I think Ms. Hightower did so. And when this man threw her to the curb, like yesterday's menu at a restaurant, she stood in the house and tried to upkeep it. She withheld and withstood and upheld the martial vows. Not because there was anything to gain in it for her, but because it's what she had committed to do.

And it's my impression, Judge, that Dori Hightower sought to honor the commitment to this marriage as a way almost personally atoning for bad judgment she'd engaged in in being snuckered by what amounts to a high rank con man.

And I cannot tell you how deeply I regret the fact that Dennis Hightower didn't have the courage or the integrity to appear in this court to withstand cross-examination. Because what I see in these documents makes my blood boil. This is a man who systemically committed fraud to serve our country in a Deputy Secretary's position, but nonetheless, an appointed position and appeared before Congress. And candidly, is little more than a liar, a man who boasted of his efforts on behalf of the CIA and his heroism in wartime, but didn't have the nerve to appear in this courtroom and answer questions about his Guatemala property. And fought her tenaciously, for years to discover what became of the 650, is it 325, we still don't even know. Because what does

Mr. Hightower say, I don't know where my son lives, it's just not credible.

We gave you the tip of a large evidentiary iceberg in a very brief trial for you to see about the inconsistent statements he's made about Guatemala, but I don't think there should be any question, in your mind, that he had or has an interest in that property and that he's dissipated assets from the marital estate, notwithstanding the standing orders, not to do so without court permission, to one person's detriment, Dori Hightower. And we put in evidence in Plaintiff's Exhibit 1-6 the expenses she incurred for that house and I'm asking you to award each and every dime. And that's really all she's sought by way of support, she didn't seek money for food or for clothing, or for entertainment, all the things you customarily see on a financial affidavit. It was the affidavit of an honorable woman who asks merely to be made whole for honoring a commitment. This man snookered her into -- and he goes into the Obama Administration, he starts losing money, I guess, maybe, I don't know, he didn't have the audacity to come here and tell us. And he leaves her and then he's out there fishing for other women with the same old rusty bait hook, you know, I'm a wonder man and I can do these great things for you, and he's no such thing.

So the financial orders will be difficult here, you might be under the impression, Judge, that given the brevity of the marriage, even, Judge, from the date of matrimony to the date of judgment, Mr. Hightower should not receive alimony. I think Connecticut is a modified no-fault state and I think you could conclude that in this instance she was a victim. This man chose her. He groomed her. He told her what to wear and got her a stylist and gave her a credit card and said dress yourself up so you can appear on my arm at the confirmation hearing and sit just behind the camera to make me look good.

And at about the time he's doing this he's jimmying up some bogus divorce decree to satisfy other creditors to presumably keep borrowing money to live beyond his means. I'm simply outraged by this. And when she came to me to ask me to represent her I heard about the guy and I thought, oh, I don't know, you know, you know, you're an adult, you fall in love with the wrong person it's your responsibility. But the more I've listened to her and the more I listened to her testimony the more I've come to understand that what he did was he sensed a weakness in her and he played it for all it was worth. And when it was worth no more to him he discarded her like rubbish and she's not rubbish, Judge, she's an honorable member of the bar.

I wanted to say that there's no jury here and I don't know that my words will move you at all but I cannot convey to you in words more powerful than I have but I'm incurring a contempt sanction. My disregard for Mr. Hightower and what he has put her through in his inability to come to this court to defend the accusations. He knows what claims we're going to make because I remind you this case was mistried initially for reasons that aren't of importance to the Court here and Mr. Hightower heard Mrs. Hightower's testimony.

The reason he is not here in this courtroom is because he knew what she would say and he knows he cannot answer. And I'm asking you to consider an adverse inference.

So as to what we're asking for we're asking for the fees that -- or the expenses she paid for the house, the alimony, going forward for a period of three and half years, I guess is a computation if the Court were to consider it. The same alimony retroactively at the same rate as it would be given prospectively, if given at all.

And then in the financial orders Ms. Hightower has also asked for a lump sum, we're asking for that as well.

And so we're asking for a lot. And the burden will be upon Mrs. Hightower, if she gets it, to perfect the claim. But she's in a unique position to do so because she's got him in the bankruptcy court where that discovery will continue. And she has reason, and I suspect good reason, on this record, to believe that this man has fraudulently conveyed and secretly hidden assets. So please, Judge, do not be seduced by the fact that he didn't appear and to thinking that this is act of modesty, or anything other than cowardess. And do not be seduced by the fact that we cannot show the extent of his wealth. We showed who he was in the past and we believe he has a substantial earning capacity. We believe he's hidden assets.

We're asking you to be generous in your award because this is a woman who gave everything and got only suffering in return from a man who used her as a little more than a kept woman. He treated her, frankly, as a mistress and he tried to walk away from a matrimonial vow. And I think this Court needs to be mindful of the fact that one of the foundations of society is stable families and the commitment of spouses to one another to honor the commitments they make in sickness and in health to be present for one another. She deserved more than she got from Mr. Hightower and if I could get punitive damages in this case I'd ask for it. So I guess I am in an indirect way. Thank you.

(Hearing Transcript April 18, 2017 at page 53 line 9 through page 60 line 7. Please note: some typographical errors in the court transcript have been corrected.)

Attorney Pattis summed up my ordeal with Dennis F. Hightower better than I could have possibly done. His words were insightful and resonate in my mind. I am truly grateful.

Finally I am ready to put Dennis F. Hightower behind me and look forward to my days ahead in my quest to help others caught in webs.

And remember, think with your head – not with your heart.

The Players

Eddie C. Brown: Founder, Chairman and CEO of Brown Capital Management, LLC, which manages approximately $4 billion in assets and is one of the largest minority-owned investment firms in the United States. A classmate of Dennis F. Hightower at Howard University. Dennis served as a Trustee on the Board of Brown Capital Management for many years. Brown Capital Management has since removed Dennis' biography from its website.

James I. Cash, Jr.: A friend of Dennis F. Hightower and former colleague at Harvard Business School where Dennis F. Hightower taught for several years. Cash served on the Board of Microsoft, General Electric, Chubb Corporation, Veracode and Walmart. He is also a member of the Boston Celtics ownership group.

Kenneth I. Chenault: Chairman and CEO American Express. Dennis F. Hightower became acquainted with him as a fellow successful black executive. Dennis tried to get money from him but was turned down. When Dennis was late on payments on his American Express Centurion Black Card he would call Chenault. Despite the foreclosure and Dennis filing for bankruptcy, somehow he was able to maintain a Black Card for many years.

Joseph Haskins, Jr.: Chairman, President and CEO, of the Harbor Bank of Maryland and CEO since 1992 at Harbor Bankshares Corporation.

Vernon E. Jordan, Jr.: A close advisor and friend to President Bill Clinton. Jordan was a mentor to Dennis F. Hightower. Dennis stated he spoke to him about the position of Deputy Secretary of Commerce. Since January 2000, Jordan has been senior managing director with Lazard Freres & Co. LLC. Jordan has served on boards including American Express, J.C. Penney and the Dow Jones Company.

Stephen P. Kaufman: A former professor at Harvard Business School, a friend of Dennis F. Hightower and the retired chairman and CEO of Arrow Electronics, Inc. Prior to joining Arrow, Kaufman spent ten years with the international management consulting firm, McKinsey & Co.

President Barack Obama: The first African-American President of the United States. A two-term President serving from 2008 to 2016. On July 22, 2009, he nominated Dennis F. Hightower to the position of Deputy Secretary of Commerce.

Richard "Dick" Parsons: Richard Parsons served as Chairman and CEO of AOL Time Warner and Chairman of Citigroup before becoming CEO of the Los Angeles Clippers in 2014. A friend of Dennis F. Hightower, Parsons co-chaired a commission on Social Security in 2001 and worked on transition teams for New York City Mayor Michael Bloomberg and New York Governor Eliot Spitzer.

Colin Powell: Former United States National Security Advisor and a retired four-star general in the Army, Powell was the first African-American Secretary of State, serving under President George W. Bush and the first African-American to serve as Chairman of the Joint Chiefs of Staff. Powell was a friend and mentor to Dennis F. Hightower.

A. Barry Rand: A friend of Dennis F. Hightower, Rand was appointed as the American Association of Retired Persons' (AARP) first African-American Chief Executive Officer in 2009. He has since retired from that position. At the helm of one of the most powerful lobbying groups in the Unites States, he was a staunch Obama supporter and a key participant in developing and supporting Obama's health care reform. Rand chaired the Board of Trustees at Howard University while Dennis F. Hightower was on the board.

J. Paul Reason: The first African-American officer in the United States Navy to become a four-star admiral. Reason attended Howard University and married Dennis F. Hightower's cousin, Dianne Lillian Fowler and also loaned money to Dennis.

Wulf von Schimmelmann: Is a German banker and corporate director. He started his career at McKinsey & Company. He is the former CEO of Deutsche Postbank AG and an Accenture Board member with Dennis F. Hightower.

Sources: Internet and Wikipedia.

LEGAL ACTIONS

Divorce

1. Divorce - Dori B. Hightower v. Dennis F. Hightower, Bridgeport Superior Court DN# FBT-FA-11- 4037815-S

Discovery Litigation

a. Dori B. Hightower v. Dennis F. Hightower, Superior Court of the District of Columbia Civil Division, Re: Deposition of Denia Stukes Hightower , 2016 CA – 002488 2.

b. Dori Hightower v. Dennis Hightower, Superior Court of the District of Columbia Family Court Domestic Relations Branch, Docket No. 2013 DRB 705 – Re Motion for Contempt A. Barry Rand Re: Deposition, Order dated May 28, 2013

c. Eddie C. Brown – Baltimore City Circuit Court Re: Motion to Quash Subpoena, Circuit Court for Baltimore City – Civil System – Dori B. Hightower vs. Dennis F. Hightower, DN# 24C13001239
Filing date: 3/4/2013
Related persons: Joseph Haskins, Jr., Eddie C. Brown and Brown Capital Management, Inc.

d. Guatemala – Commission to take son's deposition could not be served.

Foreclosure Lawsuit Connecticut

1. Foreclosure - Retained Realty, Inc. v. Dennis F. Hightower and Dori Bye a/k/a Dori B. Hightower, et al Docket Number FST CV 12-6015799-S

2. Appellate Court Foreclosure - Retained Realty, Inc. v. Dennis F. Hightower, et al, AC 37478

3. Appeal Supreme Court of Connecticut Foreclosure - Retained Realty, Inc. v. Dennis Hightower et al. Supreme Court State of Connecticut - PSC 150139

Bankruptcy (Chapter 7)

1. In Re Dennis F. Hightower a/k/a Dennis Fowler Hightower Debtor Case No. 13-646-SMT (Chapter 7) Eugenia L. Bye v. Dennis F. Hightower. Lead BK Case: 13-00646
Date filed: 10/07/15

2. Adversary Proceeding: Derivative Action
   Dori B. Hightower, On Behalf of the Estate of Dennis Fowler Hightower v.
   Dennis Fowler Hightower. Adversary Proceeding #: 15-10023
   Date filed: 10/07/15

3. Appeal to U.S. District Court – Bankruptcy Relief of Stay Order
   Appeal Case No. 16-0091
   Date filed: 02/17/2016

Collection Actions Outstanding Debts – Washington, D.C.

1. Eugenia L. Bye v. Dennis F. Hightower and Dennis F. Hightower, In the United States
   Bankruptcy Court For the District of Columbia, Case No.: 13-00646-SMT Chapter 7

2. Eugenia L. Bye v. Dennis Fowler Hightower, Washington, D.C. 2016 CA 001822B

Confession of Judgments – Maryland

1. Eddie C. Brown v. Dennis F. Hightower, Circuit Court for Baltimore Maryland Confession
   of Judgment, Case Number: 24-C-12-006477 CJ
   November 5, 2012

2. Eddie C. Brown v. Dennis F. Hightower, Circuit Court for Baltimore Maryland Confession
   of Judgment, Case Number: 24-C-12-006476 CJ
   November 5, 2012

TIMELINE

2009

April 20 — Dennis F. Hightower and Dori N. Bye meet

May 10 — Mother's Day Gift from Dennis to Dori — a Mercedes Benz SUV

May 29 — Dennis F. Hightower signs SF – Application — a questionnaire for National Security Positions including a financial disclosure

May — Dennis asks Dori to marry him

June — Family trip to Tuscany

August 7 — Senate Confirmation of Dennis F. Hightower as U.S. Deputy Secretary of Commerce

August 20 — Dori marries Dennis. Wedding held at The Delamar, Greenwich, Connecticut

August 21 — House closing. Move in to Fleur D'Eau

December 24 — $100,000 loan from Stephen P. Kaufman to Dennis F. Hightower

2010

January 19 — $125,000 loan from Richard D. Parsons to Dennis F. Hightower

April — Dennis is hospitalized

June 4 — $50,000 loan from James I. Cash to Dennis F. Hightower

June 28 — $28,000 loan from James I. Cash to Dennis F. Hightower

July 14 — $150,000 loan from Stephen P. Kaufman to Dennis F. Hightower

August 27 — Dennis 'resigns' from the Obama Administration.

September 9 — $50,000 loan from James I. Cash to Dennis F. Hightower

November 15 — $15,000 loan from Dori's mother to Dennis F. Hightower

2011

May 5 — $25,000 loan from A. Barry Rand to Dennis F. Hightower

May 27 — $17,000 loan from Dori's mother to Dennis F. Hightower

June — Dori receives a phone call from Amaretta Stone – Dennis F. Hightower's former paramour

July 11 — Dennis F. Hightower states: "I want a divorce."

September 11 — $200,000-plus loans from Eddie C. Brown to Dennis F. Hightower

October 4 — Dennis F. Hightower first discloses his "loans" to Dori and informs her she will not receive anything from the sale of their home

October 8 — Butt-dial call from Dennis F. Hightower's cell phone while on sex date with Peaches Cobbler

October 11 — Dori calls Stamford Police

October 13 — Dori B. Hightower files for divorce

2012

April 30 — Dori B. Hightower discovers the forged divorce decree in Dennis' office

June 27 — United States Office of Government Ethics — Final OGE notice in response to Dori's Appeal under the Freedom of Information Act stating that no financial disclosure will be released which leads to the question: Does the financial statement exist?

July — Dennis F. Hightower resigns from the Board of Trustees of Brown Capital Management

July 19 — Dennis F. Hightower resigns from the Board of Accenture

October 15 — Emigrant Bank files Foreclosure Action against Dennis F. Hightower

2013

May 3 — Deposition of Eddie C. Brown, Baltimore, Maryland

May 28 — A. Barry Rand refuses to be deposed and is held in contempt and ordered to pay Dori's legal fees.

June 5 — Deposition of Stephen P. Kaufman, Boston, Massachusetts

July — Dennis F. Hightower resigns from the Board of Accenture

October 13 — Dennis F. Hightower files for Chapter 7 Bankruptcy Protection

2014

January — Dori B. Hightower files Complaint Objecting to Discharge against Dennis F. Hightower regarding failure to disclose all of his assets in the Bankruptcy

April 24 — Order Approving Debtor's Waiver of Bankruptcy Discharge filed for Dennis F. Hightower in order to avoid the adversary proceeding, admitting he signed false documents and waives his Bankruptcy Discharge. The adversary proceeding is dismissed.

2015

October 7 — Dori B. Hightower files for derivative standing in the Bankruptcy Proceeding to bring a Fraudulent Conveyance Action against Dennis F. Hightower

December 2 — Dennis F. Hightower admits in a hearing that he "lied" on the Government Forms. Judge Teale grants derivative standing of Dori B. Hightower to bring the Fraudulent Conveyance Action on behalf of the Trustee

December 22 — In a Bankruptcy Hearing, Dennis F. Hightower bids $75,000 to buy back his "personal property" from the Bankruptcy Trustee

2016

January 7 — Judge Gerard Adelman orders Connecticut divorce to proceed with trial on March 22, 2016

February 1 — Dori's mother drives into the front door, causing significant damage. She has no recollection of how the car became airborne and struck the house

February 2 — Foreclosure and Title of the house passes to Retained Realty/Emigrant Bank

February 11 — Dennis F. Hightower visits Fleur D'Eau to inspect the items he wants to purchase from the Bankruptcy Trustee for $75,000

February 12 — Dori begins moving out and informs Dennis F. Hightower's counsel

February 16 — On or about this time Dennis F. Hightower rehires Attorney Catherine P. Whelan with a $50,000 retainer, he states that he borrowed from his friend 'Merricka Garfield'

February — A Marshal directed by Dennis F. Hightower's attorney blocks Dori B. Hightower's driveway in order to try to serve her

March 3 — Eugenia L. Bye (Dori's mother) files a lawsuit against Dennis F. Hightower in Washington, D.C., to recover the $34,000 plus that she loaned to him

March 9 — The same Marshal follows Dori B. Hightower into the Courtroom in Bridgeport, Connecticut, and attempts to personally serve her despite her attorney's agreement to accept service on her behalf

March — Dennis F. Hightower attorney gives Dori's lawyer the wrong address for his son Dennis F. Hightower, Jr., in Guatemala

March 18 — Dori takes a medical leave of absence

June 8 — Dori returns to work

August 23 — Divorce trial commences before Judge Mary Sommer. A friend accompanying me to court finds a nail in her tire. My Attorney Norm Pattis also finds a nail in his tire.

August 24 — Half day of the divorce trial.

August 25 — Divorce Trial continues. Dori realizes there may be a conflict of interest with the Judge during a casual breakfast with friends.

September 16 — Dori's lawyer files a Motion for Disqualification of Judge Sommer.

September 30 — Judge Sommer disqualifies herself and a mistrial is declared.

December — The Family Law Presiding Judge in Bridgeport refers the Hightower v. Hightower divorce case to be moved from Bridgeport, CT to Middletown, CT.

2017

January — The Middletown court assigns March 21 & 22 as the new trial dates

February & March — Dori receives emails from three women Dennis F. Hightower was involved with corroborating his pattern of seduction, lies and destructive behaviors and his use of cash. Two women speculate that he is hiding money. Two of the women met him online on dating websites.

March 10 — Dennis F. Hightower fails to provide any updated financial information as required prior to the divorce trial and fails to respond to formal and informal discovery requests for the correct address of his son Dennis F. Hightower, Jr. a/k/a Denny who is believed to live in Guatemala

April 17 & 18 — Divorce trial. Dennis F. Hightower fails to appear in the divorce trial

April 19 — Dori's mother's collection case for the $36,000 gets mysteriously dismissed by the Honorable Steven M. Wellner, although Dennis F. Hightower admitted owing the debt – with a comment by the court to amend the complaint to include an allegation that Dennis F. Hightower had the ability to pay Eugenia Bye back

May 22 — Eugenia Bye's complaint is refiled to address the court's requirement that she "assert" the Defendant was, at some point, able to repay the loan. Specific references are made to the sale of his Accenture Restricted Stock Units sold in 2012 and 2013 for about $380,000

May — Bankruptcy Fraudulent Conveyance Action - A settlement is reached in which Dennis F. Hightower admits the fraudulent conveyance to his son Dennis F. Hightower, Jr. rather than having a trial. Dennis F. Hightower agrees that he will not oppose the default judgment against his son Dennis F. Hightower, Jr.

August — Bankruptcy Court enters a finding that Dennis F. Hightower's forgiveness of a certain loan in the sum of $325,000 is avoided as a fraudulent conveyance and judgment entered against Denis F. Hightower, Jr. for $325,000.

September — Finally free! On September 20, 2017 my divorce became final.

NOTE: The bankruptcy proceeding is still ongoing as of the publication date of this book.

For the latest information, go to www.smilingblind.com.

About Dori B. Hightower

Dori B. Hightower, principal and founder, The Law Office of Dori B. Hightower, LLC is based in Stamford, Connecticut. Her practice concentration is in complex and contentious matrimonial cases. The Law Office of Dori B. Hightower was honored as Litigator of the Year 2014: Solo Practice by the Connecticut Law Tribune. Hightower's compassion and sensitivity in helping her clients through a difficult and often complex process has proven to be one of her strongest assets. Attorney Hightower may be contacted at dbhightower@dbhightowerlaw.com. For more information, go to www.dbhightowerlaw.com or www.smilingblind.com.

ADORE, DEGRADE, ABANDON

The patterns of behavior observed in many psychopaths include the conquering of a challenge; the dismantling of the once adored and then the dismissal of the individual once the needs of the psychopath are met or the necessity of the person is no longer required.

The behavior is repeated over and over again and permeates conduct personally and often professionally in a psychopath's life.

Should you witness this type of behavior, I have one word of advice for you-

BEWARE!

~ Dori B. Hightower